Body Language
in Europe
Unlocking the Secrets

Horst Hanisch

Idea and text: Horst Hanisch, Bonn

English editing and translation: Thomas Schommers, Neuss

Layout: Guido Lokietek, Aachen; Horst Hanisch, Bonn

Cover: Christian Spatz, engine-productions, Cologne; Horst Hanisch, Bonn

Pictures: Horst Hanisch, Bonn

Verlag: BoD · Books on Demand GmbH, In de Tarpen 42, 22848 Norderstedt, bod@bod.de

Druck: Libri Plureos GmbH, Friedensallee 273, 22763 Hamburg

ISBN: 978-3-7693-1623-0

Body Language
in Europe
Unlocking the Secrets

Greeting (second edition)

Jürgen Weischer
President EUFH/CBS/EMS University Group, 2008

"Your mouth can lie, your body cannot."

Everybody knows the saying out of our grandma's era "First impressions are everything!"

Today, we hear more often its modification "You don't get a second chance for the first impression" or even more definite "Your mouth can lie, your body cannot."

Before you introduce yourself or say your first sentence other people have already formed their first impression and this impression counts. It determines whether it is easy or difficult to communicate with the other person.

There are more decisions made the moment you see somebody for the first time than most people can imagine. To fold one's arms, to stoop, or to have cagey eyes are signs for weakness and uncertainty. They do not support the words spoken with reliability and dependability.

Body language is not only important in conferences and business negotiations. In private life, it can demonstrate everything from trust and sympathy, to neutrality and suspicion all the way to profound aversion towards somebody.

In this book, Horst Hanisch gives precise examples as good guidelines for a self-confident appearance, for a positive nonverbal communication and he encourages gaining confidence.

The goal of this book is to give the reader a future advantage by gaining more self-confidence and to present more ideas on how to analyze or unlock the body language of other people.

This competitive advantage should be used. In order to fulfill this goal this book can be very useful.

(Horst Hanisch has worked for different universities as a rhetoric coach for quite a few years. Through his research and experience he gave thousands of our students' necessary skills and success factors.)

Jürgen Weischer, 2008

"Language is the source of misunderstandings."

Antoine Marie Jean-Baptist Roger de Saint-Exupéry, French author

(1900 - 1944)

Foreword

"To think simply is a gift from God.
To think simply and speak simply is a double gift from God."
Konrad Hermann Joseph Adenauer, German chancellor
(1876 - 1967)

Stay authentic

Dear reader,

American research done by Albert Mehrabian indicates that 93 % of all interpersonal dialog is done though non-speaking behavior – nonverbal communication.

The way we watch and observe, how we move and how we use our body to make a point will be followed and analyzed by others generally unconsciously.

Body language and spoken words complement each other and give an honest overall view to other people and to ourselves.

Sometimes we just have a feeling that the person we are talking with is not being honest but we not know how to verify it. "I do not have a good feeling!" It could be that the body is telling us something else than what we hear. Is he telling a fib or is he just insecure or perhaps nervous?

It does not matter if you are skeptical about the possibility of reading body language. It is possible.

Our goal for this book is to unlock the secrets of body language and to recognize and understand the mosaic tiles of body language and to analyze them.

Everybody who becomes intensively engaged with the subject will quickly observe just how much human body language tells us. We do not need to use this knowledge to manipulate others but we can use this knowledge have an easier conversation with everybody.

It took years to gather all required information together in order to write this book.

Out of the innumerable gestures observed, we have chosen the most important ones for the Western culture.

All pictures and text should demonstrate what body language tells us and how it usually can be interpreted.

One piece of advice up-front: I believe that it does not make sense to go through everyday life always trying to control our body language because we are afraid of other people trying to analyze our body language and manipulate us.

NO – if our "verbal" statements are honest then our "nonverbal" statements are honest as well. The new knowledge about body language can contribute to awareness about our body language.

Therefore we can train ourselves to avoid certain behaviors that generate negative interpretations; especially in important situations like a job interview.

Therefore I close this foreword with these words: I hope, dear reader that you will not only be able to supplement your knowledge of body language, but will also enjoy reading this book.

Here's to harnessing the power of body language to make the most of your personal and professional future! Have fun reading and studying this book!

Horst Hanisch

Table of Contents

10

Chapter 1

Basic Assumptions

Verbal language and nonverbal language

"Some German words are so long that they have a perspective. These things are not words, they are alphabetical processions."
**Mark Twain, US-am. author
(1835 - 1910)**

Communication – understanding between two persons

Every day we talk to other people around us. We have a conversation or just simply have a small talk. As a seminar coach, for example, we talk to you and with you a lot of the time during a seminar.

The participants listen very carefully at first, but as we continue to talk, their eye lids get heavier. It happens very seldom – but it has happened before – a participant slowly falls asleep.

If we could separate verbal and nonverbal language, more of our participants would have had problems following the coach over a longer period of time. Just imagine if you had to concentrate for six to eight hours to one person lecturing.

Impossible, right? Well, fortunately your spoken words (i.e., verbal) are connected with the unspoken (i.e., nonverbal). Speaking without speaking?

To summarize: Communication – understanding between two persons – can be done verbally (with words), paraverbal (e.g., whistling) or nonverbal (as we describe it here: body language).

Perhaps it is common to believe that the largest part of communication between two people is done through verbal communication.

In fact, it can quickly be shown that we actually can communicate much more information without words. Therefore, we conclude that we actually can speak without speaking.

Whenever two people get together, whether they know each other or not, they immediately begin to communicate with each other.

"You cannot not communicate" (Paul Watzlawick, 1921 – 2007).

Just imagine the following situations:

A stranger in an evelvator

We get in an elevator with a stranger.

We know that it is an uncomfortable situation; we begin to have an unpleasant feeling. We do not talk to each other; we stare at the floor display or the ceiling of the elevator.

We cannot escape – we are stuck in the elevator. We are standing close to each other but we are not capable of starting verbal communication with the other person.

By staring at the ceiling, we avoid eye contact and we send the signal that we are not interested in talking. Maybe we intensively watch the toes of our shoes.

That shows even more that we are in an uncomfortable situation. To look down implies certain humility and to look up indicates that we are looking for help nobody can give us in this situation.

An older lady and a punk

An older lady walks through a shopping area. A young punk comes from the opposite side and walks in the direction of the older lady.

Automatically she presses her purse tighter to her body and has a firmer grip on her cane to get a more secure pace. Yes, maybe even in order to use her walking stick as a potential weapon to defend herself.

If she would have the possibility she would even change directions to avoid a direct confrontation with the young punk.

In the subway

A guy is sitting on a bench for two people in the subway. The bench across from him is empty. A second guy enters the subway and takes a seat on the empty bench.

After quick eye contact (he's not going to do anything to me?) the first guy starts looking out the window. There is no desire for any more eye contact.

How would the person have reacted if the second guy would have requested the empty seat on the bench right next to the first guy?

Same situation in the subway. The first guy has his computer bag next to him and on the bench across from him he has a newspaper laid out and he is reading it.

Would you request one of the seats if there were other seats available in the subway?

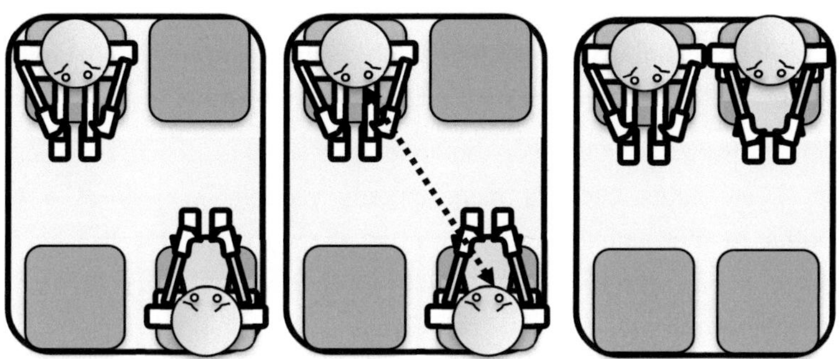

Without speaking directly to the other persons, our examples show through nonverbal communication what the individuals want, what they do not want or what they are afraid of. Everybody knows several situations like that.

Nonverbal communication allows us to act freely and secure in society. Without speaking, other people understand what we want, wish, feel, or what we are afraid of.

These examples demonstrate how broad nonverbal communication is and how important this kind of communication is for inter-personal relationships.

Seven seconds and four minutes

Did you know that after a maximum of seven seconds (7!) you have made the decision whether you like somebody or not? These are seven seconds where you most likely have not spoken a word.

When you need information at the train station platform: Who do you ask? The first person that you see?

Did you know that a recruiter knows after four minutes (4!) in a job interview whether you get a job offer or not?

When you meet somebody for the first time most of your communication will be nonverbal. Imagine you meet somebody you have not seen before in a hotel lobby.

You walk up to him, smile and then reach out to shake his hand with your first words. Realize how fast the first few seconds are gone.

Before you begin to talk to your audience as a speaker, coach, or lecturer, most likely some seconds have already passed; sometimes a few minutes. At that point, the audience has already decided if they have a positive or negative feeling about you. All that without you even saying one single word!

Therefore it is very important to avoid any kind of body movements that could cause negative connotations; especially at the beginning of a speech.

During the conversation or presentation almost everybody who has certain skills can verbally persuade the audience.

Just as the audience can interpret the nonverbal body language of the speaker within seconds, the speaker also can do the same with the audience.

This way the person presenting is able to quickly develop a very important impression of the audience. Is their attitude more likely positive or negative? Are they aggressive and waiting for the first attack?

Answering these questions is essential for survival.

It would not have been the first time that a well-educated and trained coach or entertainer failed in front of the audience because he did not interpret the body language of his audience at all or he interpreted it incorrectly.

We do not want that to happen to you and therefore we will unlock and explain many nonverbal signals of body language.

Of course, nonverbal communication also happens between two people who simply talk to each other, who meet in an elevator, or who negotiate a sale.

Does body language lie?

We recognize that body language existed long before the spoken word. Therefore, reactions inside our body and with our body are automatic, excitable, and unconscious.

Research has verified that certain reactions are the same all over the world and that they are also interpreted the same!

We can expect that body language tells us the truth, unless it is manipulated to indicate something else. Verbally we can say that it rains even if we have wonderful weather with a shining sun and blue sky.

It is pretty easy: we fib or even worse, we lie.

If somebody is cold, then he will start to protect his body. Through shivering, folding his arms across his chest, or rubbing his hands, he will create heat.

If we see somebody doing this, then we can expect that this person is cold. He is not faking.

Most nonverbal communication therefore comes from inside. Some bodily reactions such as growing and pupil dilatation cannot be influenced.

We conclude: If the body language of our counterparty is unconscious, we can expect that it is honest and real.

Suggestions for analyzing body language

As an acknowledgement: we are not able to say that all circumstances are the same. The reason simply is that every situation is different and everybody also reacts differently.

We do not need to be scared off or hope that we can analyze or judge someone just because of his body language.

If we add the spoken words, it may be possible for some specialists, but for the ordinary and average human beings, what is important is that we can just analyze and judge certain behaviors.

We always should have in mind that we are human and that means that we can also misinterpret situations.

Additionally, it is impossible to just take a small section of human behavior and use it as a sample to draw absolute conclusions for all human behavior.

To draw that conclusion, the interaction of all muscles within the human body is too complex.

Never-ending interaction

Just imagine you want to drink a sip of water out of a glass on your desk.

It is impossible to just take the water glass without making sure with your eyes where exactly the glass is situated on your desk.

As you pick up the water glass you will control the action through your eyes. That means that the motor function of your hand and the movement of your eyes work together.

In order to put these two actions into practice we will absorb, process, and analyze them all at the same time.

If we just look at the eyes we cannot know that the hand picked up a glass. Also when we move the hand with the glass to our mouth another reaction happens in our brain and our mouth: we can observe the movement of our lips.

Finally, we need to open our mouth a little bit so we can put the glass to our lips to drink.

We can imagine the never-ending interaction between our senses and body parts as well as the use of devices or the surrounding area that might be in order to achieve successful goals.

And there are thousands of goals like that during an average day.

To unlock the secrets of body language we need to realize again and again the following guideline in order to avoid a wrong interpretation:

Body language can only be unlocked if the behavior symbolizes a reaction to an action.

What does that mean? Well, we act by saying or doing something that others react to. Only at that moment it is possible to correctly interpret the reaction.

For example: Somebody with arms crossed in front of his chest sitting before us does not necessarily mean that he does not like us.

Maybe he is just not to keen about the new surrounding area; maybe he is cold or maybe he has a physical impairment so he has to sit like that.

It is impossible to have a definite analysis!

But: if we say or do something and then the other person crosses his arms in front of his chest we can be sure that it is a reaction to our action and it is possible to clearly analyze it!

Criteria of perception

How many people believe that they have correct posture?

From a subjective point of view, that might be right but from an objective point of view, it might not be the case.

The posture of human beings is controlled by our skeleton and muscles. Therefore it happens though our subconscious mind.

When we monitor our expressions we realize that our posture could intuitively reflect our mood.

People with an erect posture walk straight through life; they know what they want.

They are standing with their feet on the ground, nothing can change their opinion, and they are energetic and persuasive.

They abandon themselves to their grief.

How would you interpret the posture of the following people?

And ... before you keep on reading, please point out applicable characteristics of the two persons below:

Person 1	Person 2

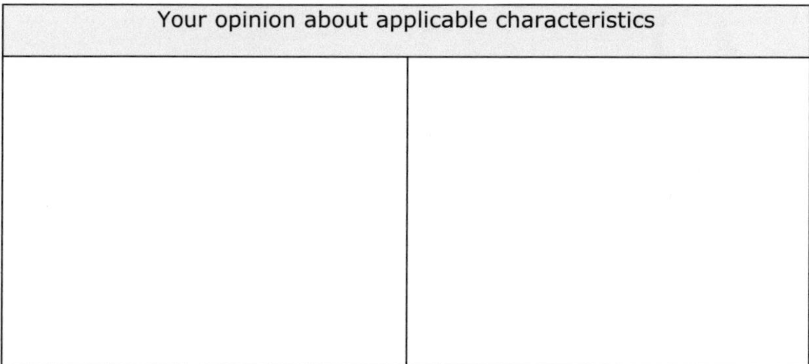

Your opinion about applicable characteristics	

It is not possible to have a definite interpretation. But it is possible to have an interpretation which is most likely.

Observation of the first person	
	• stand with both feet apart on the ground • straight posture • both arms are outstretched from the shoulders • shoulders slightly pulled in
Observation of the second person	
	• backbone slouched • arms are down and behind the back • hands are behind the back • head and (therefore) eyes looking down • feet close together

Possible interpretation (second person):

• depressed, a person slightly bowing down	• does not have his own opinion
• does not show readiness for action	• always agrees with everything ("yes-man") and therefore people like to take advantage of him
• wants to back out of something	• he is not a successful person

▪ is shy	▪ does not know what to do
▪ he holds his head down and tucked in to analyse the situation and, if necessary, back off quickly	▪ undecided, questioning
▪ constrained	▪ not proactive, is afraid of making decisions
▪ avoids eye-contact and therefore gets characterized as bashful, inhibited or not telling the truth	▪ hides behind the opinions of other people
▪ has few friends	▪ always waits for the perfect situation and is never the first one to present his own opinion
▪ modest	▪ self-conscious (self-doubt), may have a pessimistic attitude toward life

Normally, our sense and sensibility match the characteristics. We perceive through our sub-consciousness who is in front of us.

Charisma

Without even talking to somebody, we analyze other people.

We should not forget that it takes no more than seven seconds to form an opinion about somebody we have met. We do that because of our experience in life and without even saying one single word to the new person.

Understandably, we adopt a certain behavior towards other people or we change it depending on the impression we have about that particular person.

Humometer

It is possible to compare it with our internal thermometer every human being has. Let's call this inside thermometer "*humometer.*"

Before we meet somebody for the first time our *humometer* towards this person is neutral.

Therefore it has 0° and is balanced out.

When the charisma or appearance of the new person is more likely positive to us, our *humometer* will display a positive green sphere.

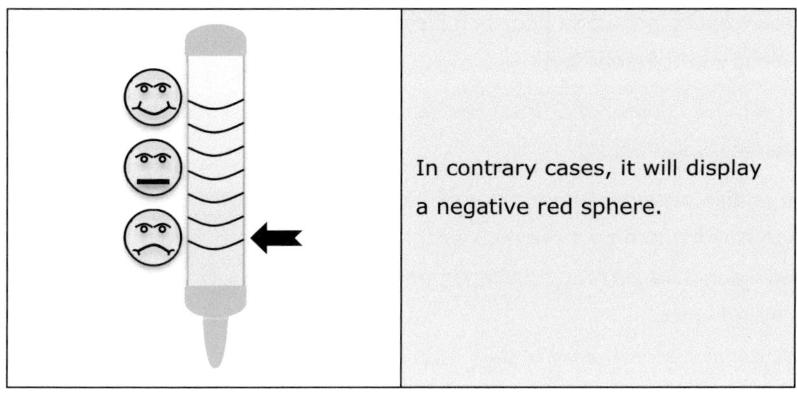

In contrary cases, it will display a negative red sphere.

Which of the two people will persuade us to do something more readily? The one on the right side or the one on the left side?

25

Well, of course the person on the left side.

The green position

The green position of the person makes us believe that the statements of this person are positive and we are grateful for his opinions. The scale on our *humometer* rises.

Just imagine yourself as a coach: all your participants have a *humometer* in their minds and wait excitedly for your appearance.

Your goal as a coach is to create a positive atmosphere.

You want to persuade your participants about your comments as well as about your personality.

The more "green" the first impression is, the more successful your conversation will be.

It is also possible to start out of the red scale. Maybe your participants are still irritated by a previous speaker and, therefore, you may start out with negative surrounding conditions or a negative framework you could not influence.

That means that the situation you have to start out with is on the red scale.

Of course it is possible through our charisma to navigate the participants into a neutral or positive *humometer*-position and maybe later even into the green scale. But it takes quite a bit of effort and energy – physical and mental. It also can be time consuming.

It could have happened to you before that you were not able to bring your participants back into the green scale. For all persons involved, it is an unpleasant and unsatisfying situation.

It is likely that there could be harsh criticism. The participants will block and boycott the coach in every possible situation.

It will be an uphill battle against the coach which he has to lose and will lose. In a situation like this specialized knowledge is useless.

Facial expression

Facial expressions are very meaningful. It occurs very often and very quickly. There are many muscles in the face of a human being which interact.

It is said that, especially with older people, facial expressions tell you how they lived their lives. Is that true? We all know the luminous yellow Smiley. Just one circle, two dots and one curved line for a mouth.

Let's look closely at the Smiley. What kind of feelings does the Smiley create inside you?

Before you keep on reading, please write down your notes.

What did you fill in?

What kind of feelings did you get when you looked closely and thoughtfully at the Smiley?

I felt:

▪ secure, calm	▪ accepted as human being
▪ friendly	▪ positive influence
▪ approved of	▪ happy, lucky
▪ welcomed	▪ full of life or joys

All that just because of a face made out of lines and dots (i.e., not even a whole person made out of lines and dots).

To make it complete and to demonstrate the difference here is the second Smiley.

The line for the mouth was just turned upside down. What happens is that we get an entirely new picture. Look closely at this face and think about how it affects you.

Maybe you say that it did not mean anything different to you. But you think that such a statement is unbelievable, correct?

Do you want to deal with somebody who acts like the second Smiley towards you? Do you think that the people you talk to want to work together with you if you radiate the same atmosphere and charisma?

Smiling disarms

A simple smile pulls your participants into the green scale! It is easier to sell our ideas (or topics, goods, services and so on) if we smile.

Smiling disarms!

Just because of an interpreted attitude of the mouth, which is displayed to us by a simple curved line of the Smiley, we develop different feelings.

Therefore, think the face of a human being with all its unlimited nuances and facial expressions that it can create and how much potential can be realized.

If we walk with a persuasive and confident attitude through life, our facial expression will demonstrate our success.

When we negotiate with a potential customer, we will achieve better contract conditions than our competitors! This won't be just one time, this will be all the time, our entire (employed) life. Successful conversations are almost guaranteed!

Physiognomy (facial expression)

If we believe the scientists Duisky and Psypich, when people look at a picture of a person, they form a distinct (determined, energetic, decisive) preconception (first impression) after ¼ of a second.

This perception is emotional. The person seems to be friendly, authoritarian, malicious, intelligent, boring, etc.

Even after a longer reflection, the first impression does not or rarely changes. In comparison to a picture, a film of a person should influence an observer even stronger (source: Spiegel 50/99).

A quarter of a second appears to be not much time. Other research indicates about 2 to 3 seconds, or even 7 seconds. We will stay with the relatively high assumption of 7 seconds.

It takes a maximum of only seven seconds for someone to decide whether he likes the person he is looking at or not.

Only seven seconds! Frequently, much is riding on these seven seconds: making the sale, getting the job, or simply creating a positive atmosphere amongst the people who surround us at our jobs or in our private lives. These seconds correspond with the first impression that the person opposite us has of us.

No second chance to make a first impression

We never get a second chance to make a first impression! This is why these seven seconds are so extraordinarily important for us.

Business partners, customers and guests expect much more from today's employees than merely professional knowledge and skills. The personal touch is increasingly in demand; interpersonal skills that are in step with the times often make the difference in closing the deal.

Did you know that, in a job interview, the decision on whether to hire the candidate is made in the mind of the interviewer after only four minutes?

This shows us that the human component evidently has a very strong influence on the person we're speaking to.

First impressions can of course be deceiving. Perhaps the person is not really what he appears to be. But what's important is that we have a maximum of seven seconds to make an impression.

And from our own point of view – subjectively – the first impression corresponds to reality. In these first seconds, we have already judged the person to be sincere, self-conscious, friendly, self-assured, sales-oriented, etc.

The results of research demonstrate that people (on a picture), who lower their head are more likely seen as humble, and people who raise their head, as arrogant or presumptuous.

Certainly, we are human and therefore we form a first impression – we are not a computer, which operates without feeling and is unemotional.

There is a danger or risk of misinterpretation. It is possible that we get a wrong – maybe absolutely incorrect – impression of a person.

Therefore, the ability to follow any such conversation is not optimal.

Face-to-face interaction, eye-contact

Through the eyes we see the inside of human beings. Is that true?

Well, eyes tell us a lot. They can shine; they can appear to be dry. They can look questioning, inquisitive, pushy, dreaming, in love, evil …

The pupils are wide or narrow; the eyes are in slits or wide open.

If we keep eye-contact with others we show candour and thoughtfulness.

If our eyes look to the ground it can be interpreted as constraint, shy, sadness, or even that you are trying to lie to somebody.

"He cannot look into my eyes."

When the face-to-face interaction is fixed for too long, it can make others uncomfortable. We will get nervous or aggressive. The other one has more strength or is more powerful.

As a speaker, we should establish the eye-contact with everybody in our audience if possible in order to keep our communication connected but we should not be fixed on one person all the time because we do not want to disturb him.

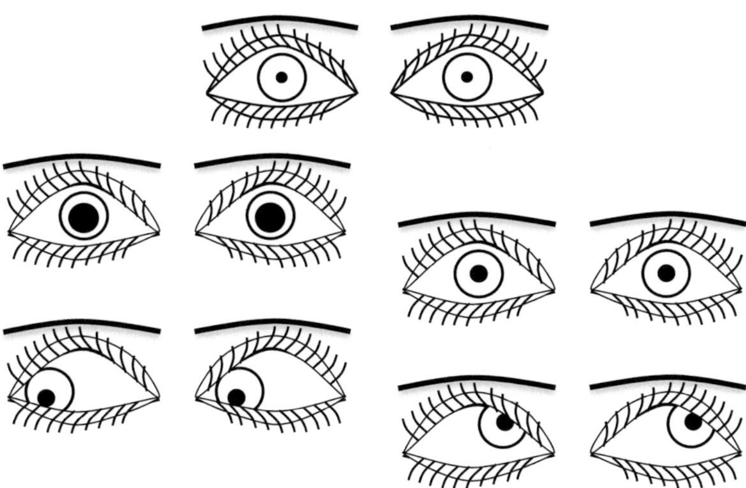

Gestures, motor functions

The composition of all looks and movements are called gestures. Parts of gestures are the movement of your arms, legs and your head.

Motor functions are defined as the precise movement of body parts, e.g., the movement of a finger while you pick up a mug or when you are holding a pencil.

Using your finger to write some text is called fine motor skills. Thumb and index finger unite an infinite number of neurons.

Besides the temperature we can absorb different characteristics by stroking the surface of an area. Is the surface made out of stone, wood, or cloth? Is it even, rough, or coarse? Dry or wet? Are there bread crumbs or dust balls?

In order to "realize" things we need to touch them. There is a reason why we frequently hear desperate cries of young mothers in shops:

• "… keep your fingers off … "	• "… just watch with your eyes … "
• "… don't touch … "	• „… just look, don't grab …"

Our fingers and our hands are extremely important to comprehend and to understand the world. Therefore, we can often explain and say with our hands much more than with our spoken words.

Spiral stairs

Ask somebody to explain what spiral stairs are. In almost all cases the person will trace the spiral stairs with his fingers.

That is more expressive, more secure, and wiser than trying to explain it with our complicated language.

Hands support our statements. Do you know the fisherman who caught "such a big fish"?

In some cultures using your arms is extremely integrated in the spoken language. Just imagine an Italian who describes a pretty person or appetizing food.

In our culture, sometimes we have problems to use our hands to support the spoken words. That also means that our presentation will be seen as callous and, therefore more difficult to understand.

A trained person will use gestures selectively to make verbal expressions more understandable and therefore more graphic. In order to respect the persons we talk to we should avoid to fidgeting in front of them.

It is not a secret anymore that restraining our hands and arms during a conversation blocks the function of our brain. The function of our brain and the movement of our arms have a direct influence on each other.

33

Nonverbal questions and answers

As a speaker, our goal should be to satisfy the needs and wants of our audience. If we do not make our point clear to the participants, then we have missed our goal.

Therefore we should always analyze our audiences' responses towards our speech or presentation and ask ourselves the questions: "Did the audience understand what I was talking about? Was I unclear with the words and expressions I used?"

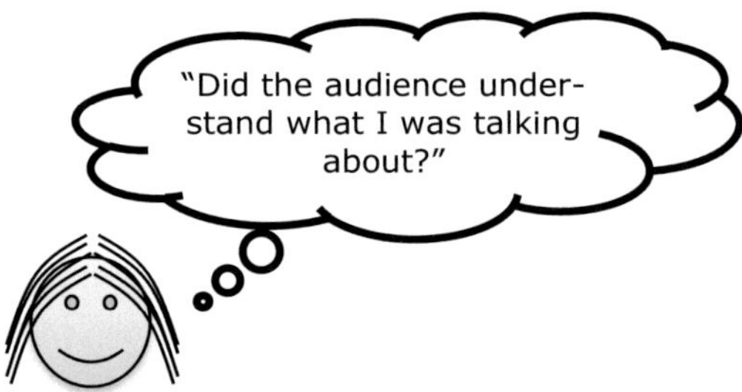

Well-known nonverbal question and answer are the following for example:

• shrug the shoulders and maybe to look to the side at the same time • "I don't know, don't ask me."
• raise the eyebrows and frown • "Is it really true? Is that right?"
• nod the head • "Yes, that's right. I experienced this in a similar situation. I totally agree."
• lower the head • "Is that really right?"

- knit one's brows together by squeezing the eye-brows together

- "Please explain that one more time to me."

- moving of the eyes to the side to a third person and to twist the eyes

- "The other person seems to be a little bit crazy."

Body language and its secrets – what it tells you and how you can analyze it or unlock it.

There are almost 300 pictures following and with these pictures it is possible to unlock the meaning of the body language.

Finally, body language won't be such a secret anymore.

35

What creates the first impression?

What elements contribute to creating the first impression? Let's make a list of what we've already mentioned:

• Age	• Clothing (neat, modern, clean, color)
• Appearance	• Hair (Color, neat, short, long)
• Jewelry (Glittering like a Christmas tree? Pierced in all possible and impossible body parts? Fashion jewelry or no jewelry at all?)	• Make-up (Applied appropriately to accentuate the personality, or more like a mask?)
• Demeanor (Self-assured or self-conscious?) Eye contact (Eyes cast humbly downward? Looking upward, bored? Looks us directly in the eye? A smile on the lips? Smiles can be disarming!)	

These are only a few of the points that can influence the first impression we make. But please note: you are not the only one who is receiving these signals and using them to form your first impression of others. No!

Possibly even more importantly: your listeners or dialogue partners are also receiving signals from you. Do you think that a listener who has the impression that you're bored, stuck-up, tired, frustrated, angry etc. will want to have anything to do with you?

Do you think that, after this kind of impression, a sales pitch has any chance of succeeding?

Body distance

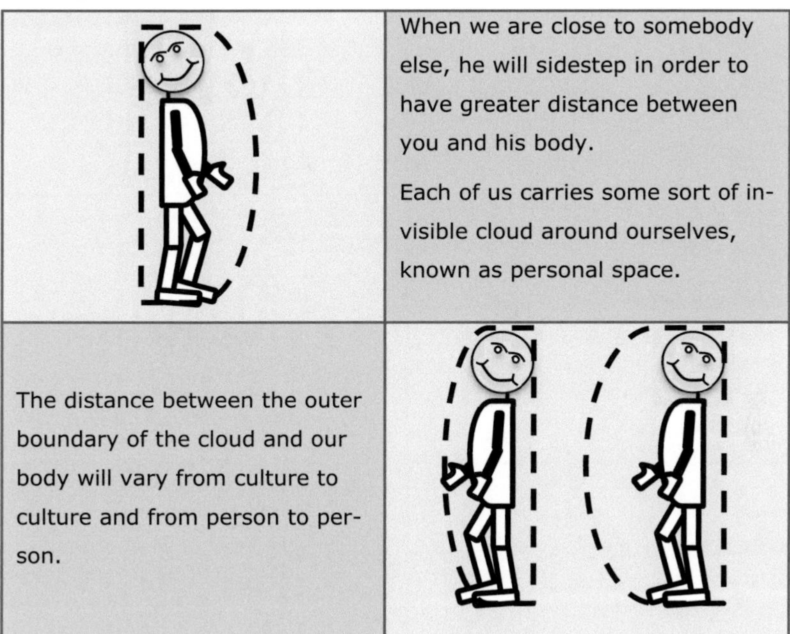

	When we are close to somebody else, he will sidestep in order to have greater distance between you and his body. Each of us carries some sort of invisible cloud around ourselves, known as personal space.
The distance between the outer boundary of the cloud and our body will vary from culture to culture and from person to person.	

Usually it is in between zero and 70 centimeters. Zero means the direct contact with another person.

Personal space is a distance we can easily defend with our arms. Whenever two people talk to each other, each of them will respect the personal space of the other one.

Therefore both people stand like this: The outer boundaries of the clouds touch each other; a very good exchange of thoughts is possible.

If one of the people gets too close to the other, the situation would appear as follows:

Usual distance	
One person invades the other person's personal space. This person will feel uneasy and, if possible, will step back. An exchange or trade is not possible.	
Usual distance is given again.	

We all know how uncomfortable it is if somebody invades in our personal space. Remember the situation in the elevator.

Here, we do not have spacious conditions and therefore we cannot respect the needed and wanted distance. That is the reason why we stare at the ceiling or the floor display.

We try to avoid eye-contact because we do not want aggressions to rise. We are glad when the elevator reaches the floor we wanted and we can leave.

Personal space

In certain situations, we have to accept that somebody invades our personal space. Sometimes it is to the extreme whereby someone touches our body, such as visiting a doctor, a masseuse, or hair dresser, etc.

Touching our body is a violation of our personal space. We just permit such an action for persons with whom we are intimately close to.

The only reason why we can accept work-related invasions into our personal space is that we consider this person to be a *persona non grata.*

If a person does not want to provoke aggression in a conversation he should make sure to respect the personal space of the other person. It is taboo to touch somebody else's body.

To touch each other and to break this taboo is just accepted through hand-shakes by greeting and saying good-bye to somebody.

A person who is sitting will always have problems to accept help from somebody who is standing and leaning over him.

The person standing appears to be authoritative or overbearing.

Beside the personal space we also recognize territorial space.

Within our private life the territorial space includes our home, our yard, or our balcony as well as our car and a short distance around our car.

We need this territory in order to manage and survive in our daily life without problems. Therefore our workplace and our working desk belong to this territorial space.

The desk belongs to this territorial space because that is the place where we store and sort our paperwork and we need this space in order to work or learn.

Therefore it is not advisable to lean on somebody else's desk or, even worse, to sit on it when we want to have a successful conversation with him. This is an invasion into his territorial space and therefore viewed negatively.

If you do not give others the opportunity to build up his own personal space the person will react very careful, observant, or even constrained.

Some people want to have exactly this situation because they use this to their advantage and will have the stronger or more powerful position.

If we consider the *humometer,* we realize that it is more difficult to appear positive at the beginning of a conversation in such a starting situation.

Tone of voice – paraverbal communication

We all know that there are different ways of speaking and that they have an incredible influence on our verbal statements and naturally on the person we are talking to as well.

When we speak we can choose to use a monotonous tone to put others to sleep. The person listening will certainly appreciate it because soon he will be released from listening to us by falling asleep!

Just imagine this tone of voice over a longer time period. Drone. Just like the contents of a contract or agreement?

A monotone voice does not have increasing and decreasing tones. The more constant the tone of voice, the more exhausting it sounds to the persons listening.

On the other side, a wavelike tone of voice with quiet the some increasing and decreasing tones will more likely remind us of a church than of a dynamic speech or an impressive presentation.

41

Tone of voice should be dynamic

Therefore, we conclude that our tone of voice should be dynamic.

Typical for a dynamic tone of voice is an irregular intonation, sometimes louder to underline a statement and sometimes soft-spoken or quiet to beg for attention.

Sometimes we speak quickly and sometimes slowly.

The diversity of tones of voices reflects the multiplicity of the subject. The audience is listening attentively because they cannot know what happens next.

That is the main difference from other mentioned tones of voice. Therefore it is advisable to have breaks within a fluent speech or presentation.

They have a positive influence on the ability to concentrate on the subject for the audience.

Of course we should articulate everything clearly as well. The best information is useless if we mumble or if we use incomprehensible words.

We bring life into our spoken words. Our subject is up to date and alive. It is oriented on our expressiveness of our explanations:

Sometimes

▪ factually – precise – concluding	▪ amused – hilarious
▪ inquiring – doubtful	▪ ironic – sarcastic
▪ sorrowful	▪ descriptive

"Descriptive" means that we make a verbal statement visually through nonverbal communication.

In order to do that, we use our huge repertoire of body language.

The more emotional our tone of voice is the more significant and emotional is the behaviour and response of our audience!

Chapter 2

Unlocking the secrets of body language: The head

2.1 Mouth, lips, tongue

2.1.1 Smiling

A smile disarms. This person is in a good mood (about the situation and the other person).

Here it is a genuine smile that is coming from inside (compared with 2.3.1: *The forced Smile*).

The corners of the mouth are slightly drawn up. Slight creases are formed underneath the eyes.

2.1.2 Fanning air to the mouth

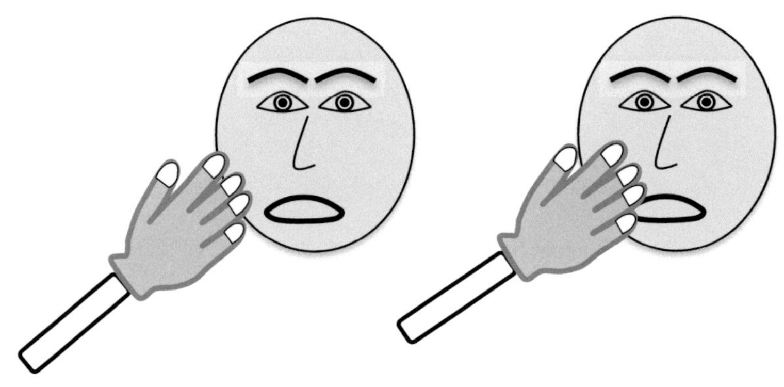

The person just burned his mouth with hot food or a hot drink. In order to relieve the pain he fans cool air to his mouth.

It is also possible to use this gesture when somebody burned his tongue to demonstrate sympathy.

Air is fanned to the mouth with one hand.

2.1.3 Covering the mouth with one hand

The person refuses to use his mouth because he just said something he should not have or would not want to say by holding his hand over his mouth.

"Oh, no, I shouldn't have said that."

At the same time the person is surprised about his own behavior or scared about his own candor.

One hand quickly covers the mouth and the thumb is tucked to the side of the nose.

45

2.1.4 Slightly drawing down the corners of the mouth

The person demonstrates his displeasure.

It also can be a sign of a lack of interest, or ignorance.

"I don't know."

Or: "I don't care."

The corners of the mouth are slightly drawn down.

2.1.5 Poking the tongue out

He is poking his tongue out to someone else.
That means that he wants to offend and does
not respect him/her.

This gesture can be judged very negatively.
Perhaps a conversation to clear up the situation is necessary and advisable.

Sometimes this gesture is used as a joke or
to be funny.

Be careful when you use this gesture toward
superiors in your organization because it is
possible that is interpreted as questioning
their authority!

The tongue pokes out toward the other person.

2.1.6 Poking the tongue out to the side

You can see this kind of gesture sometimes
when somebody is concentrating or pondering
over an exercise or assignment.

The tongue pokes a bit out to the side.

2.1.7 Licking the lips

The person wets the lips by rubbing the tongue over the lips. "Hmm, I really like that."

This kind of gesture is often associated with sexual thoughts.

Licking the lips once or several times.

2.1.8 The open mouth

To open the mouth and keep it open for several seconds demonstrates speechlessness.

"I don't know what I should say about that."

The person is absolutely surprised about what somebody just said or done.

The mouth opens and stays open for a short period of time (several seconds).

2.1.9 Speaking quieter and slower

The person speaks quieter and slows down as he speaks.

It shows that he lost his concentration and that he is not as firm about the subject any more.

He shows uncertainty and weakness.

He will continue speaking quieter and slower.

2.1.10 Pressing lips together

The person does not want to or cannot say anything.

He presses his lips together so that no thoughtless words accidently spill out.

Extreme interpretation: he is holding back his anger. He is balky and it is not possible to satisfy, persuade, or convince him.

The lips are pressed tightly together.

2.1.11 Biting the lips

The person has his lips closed to gain some time to consider an opinion or thought.

He is contemplative but also unconfident. He bites on his lips so that he does not have to say anything.

Slightly closed lips are bitten.

2.1.12 Touching the lower lip with the index finger

The person points with his index finger on the lower lip of his mouth.

He wants to say: "I want to talk to you."

Or: "Can I talk to you in private/confidence?"

Pointing the index finger of one hand several times on the bottom lip.

2.1.13 Lifting the upper lip

When he lifts up his upper lip you can see his teeth. That can be interpreted as a threat or a sign of power or strength.

This demonstrates disregard or contempt toward the other person.

This kind of gesture or behavior is not good for the situation because obviously this is not helpful for a sense of community, a corporate identity, or for solidarity.

The upper lip is pulled up.

2.1.14 Pulling up the lower lip

Here the mouth is closed by pulling up the lower lip. The person does not want to say something accidently or inappropriate.

This kind of gesture demonstrates skepticism towards what has been said or done.

The lower lip is pulled up over the upper lip.

2.1.15 Holding a hand in front of the mouth

The person behaves reserved, maybe he is even constrained. He could say something but he does not have the heart to do so. The speaker could ask him to contribute his opinion in the discussion.

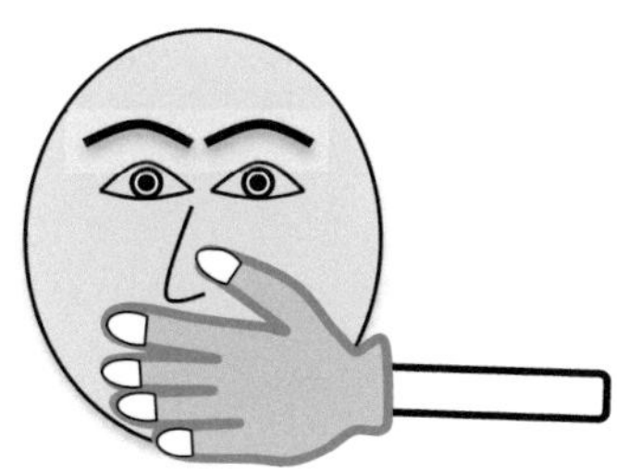

One hand is held across the mouth. The fingertips are parallel to the lips. The thumb may be held up.

2.1.16 Exaggerated smile

By lifting up the corners of the mouth you can
see the person's teeth.

It demonstrates to us that this person is
ready to act or is aggressive.

The person is self-confident and believes he is
in a superior position compared to his counter
party.

He is teasing, or even ridicules his counter-
party.

Both corners of the mouth are turned up.

The mouth is open a little bit so you can see the teeth.

2.1.17 The forced Smile

In general, smiling gives a positive impression
and it disarms.

Sometimes lifting up the corners of the mouth
seems to be artificial because there are no
creases around the eyes (compare 2.1.1:
Smiling).

The so-called forced smile suggests closeness
and acceptance.

If the person is gently shaking his head, he
indicates that he is skeptical.

The corners of the mouth are slightly drawn up.

2.2 Eyes

2.2.1 The eyes wide open

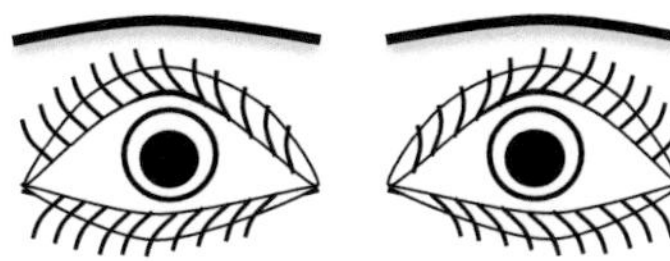

The person shows disbelief.

"Is that really true?"

Or: "I can't believe that."

The counter-party should reconsider the subject from a different point of view in order to make it clearer.

Both eyes are wide open and the eyebrows lifted up.

2.2.2 Squinting eyes

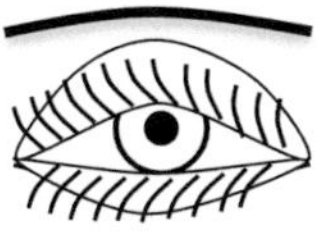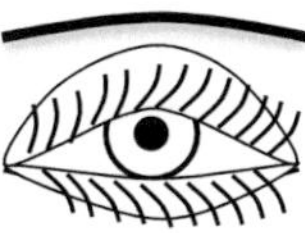

The person shows disbelief: "Well, if that is really true what he is talking about?"

It is also possible that the person strains his eyes because the sunlight.

Both eyelids are pressed close together so that the eyes are halfway closed.

51

2.2.3 Eyes looking up and to the left

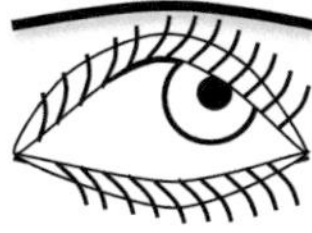

A right-handed person tries to remember something (in his left side of the brain).

He is searching for something that is already memorized.

For a left-handed person this is reversed.

Both eyes look from the person's perspective up and to the left.

2.2.4 Eyes looking up and to the right

A right-handed person tries to remember something (in the right side of his brain).

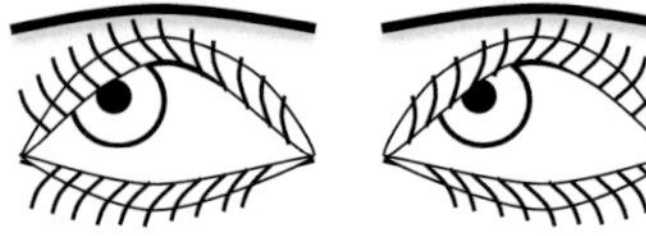

He is searching for something that seems to be fantasy.

This gesture can be noticed when somebody is telling a fictional story or describing a fact pictorially with the words: "Just imagine ..."

For a left-handed person this is reversed.

Both eyes look from the person's perspective up and to the right.

2.2.5 Eyes looking to the left

A right-handed person is searching for memories in the left side of his brain.

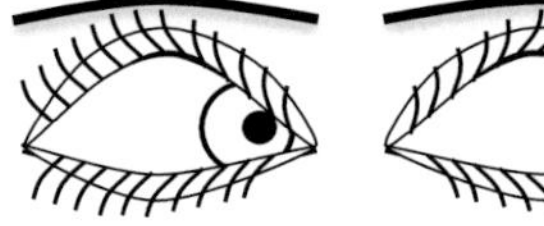

He is especially looking for memorized tones, sounds, and noises.

For a left-handed person this is reversed.

Both eyes look from the person's perspective to the outside left

2.2.6 Eyes looking down and to the left

A right-handed person is searching for memories in the left side of his brain.

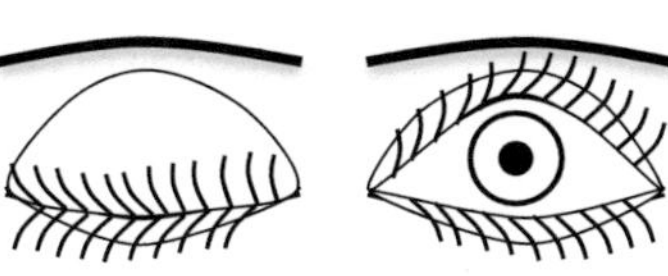

He is especially looking for memorized aromas, smells, and odours.

Gesucht wird speziell nach gespeicherten Gerüchen.

For a left-handed person this is reversed.

Both eyes look from the person's perspective down and to the left.

2.2.7 Winking one eye

53

The person demonstrates to the other person "secretly" that he has the same opinion: "Well, we will get along very well."

Through this action they form a secret pact: "We both know something the others don't know."

Winking once with one eye to send a signal to the other person.

2.2.8 Wandering eyes

In general the person has interest in the subject but he does
not have the heart to look into
the eyes of his conversation
partner.

It shows concerns and uncertainty.

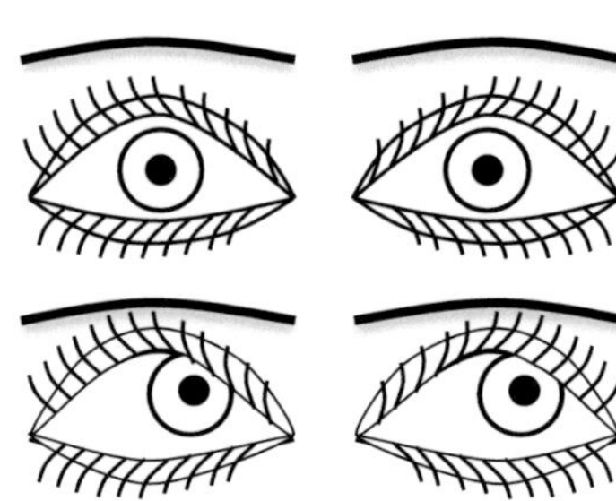

It is possible that there are details about the subject that the person
does not want to discuss.

Both eyes are moving nervously or anxiously around the room.

2.2.9 Eyes looking up

The person his seeking for help
from a higher being: "God,
please help me!"

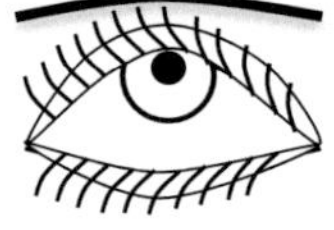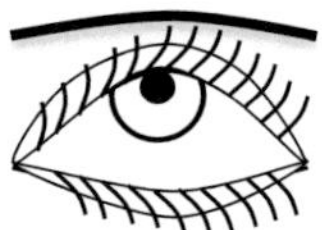

It also is possible that the person is making fun of the other person:
"Oh my God! What did you say again?"

Both eyes are looking directly up toward the sky.

2.2.10 Nearly closed eyes

The eyes are nearly closed and
they are looking down. The head
is slightly turned down as well.

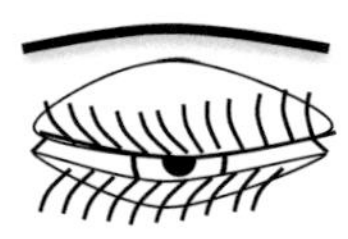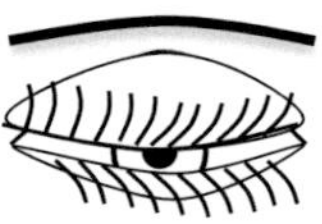

This gesture can be interpreted as a position of humility. The person
wishes to comply with the other person.

Through closing the eyes this gesture sends a strong statement. The
person shows uncertainty: "I'm innocent. Please leave me alone."

Both eyes are nearly closed and looking down.

2.2.11 Closing eyes and lifting up eyebrows

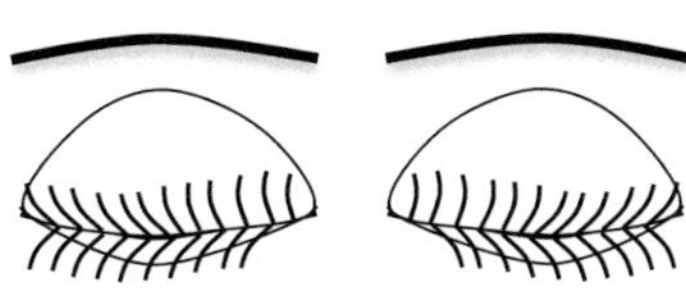

This illustrates an arrogant, uppity, and snobbishly gesture.

The person demonstrates clearly that he stands above the others and that he does not care about the subject.

Both eyes are closed.

The eyebrows are lifted up high.

2.2.12 Looking to the side

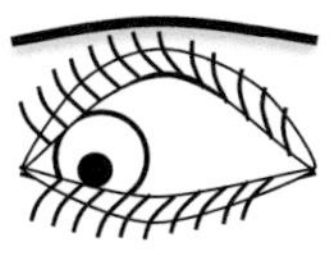 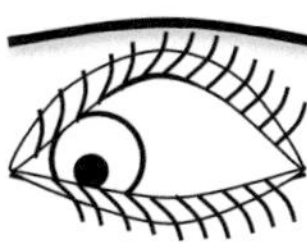

The person shows a position of humility. By lowering the head this gesture is even stronger.

He demonstrates that he cannot look into the eyes of the other person because of shyness, humility, or awe.

The eyes are looking to the side and the head is lowering and turning as well.

2.2.13 Staring

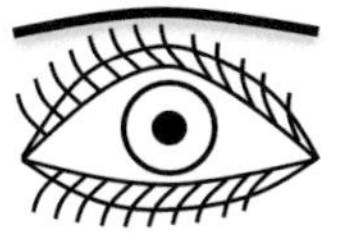 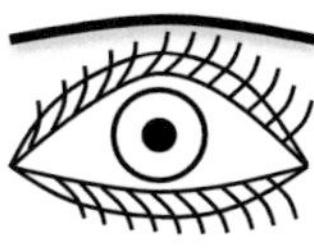

The person demonstrates his own awareness and that he does not let himself get shocked and awed.

He also shows strength and power and, yes – he is trying to shock and awe the other people as well.

The person who looks away first has lost, and has the weaker position.

Both eyes are staring at the other person.

If possible, without batting an eye.

2.2.14 Lifting up one eye-brow

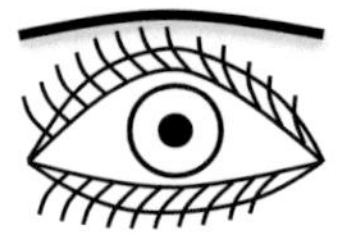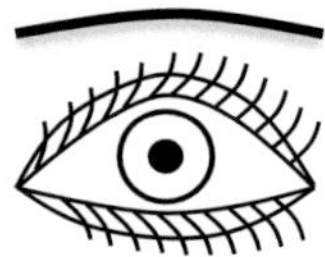

The person is skeptical about the explanations and remarks of the speaker.

The speaker should be prepared for a confrontation within a short period of time.

"Well, I have a completely different opinion/position."

Or: "Well, I have heard/read something completely different."

One eyebrow is lifted up.

2.2.15 Lifting up both eye-brows

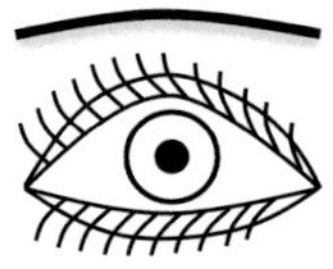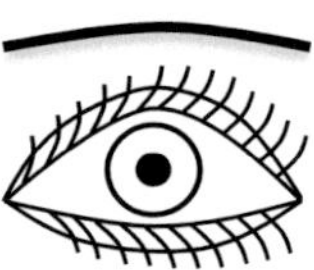

Lifting up both eyebrows for a moment increases the area around the eyes.

The person saw somebody he knows and he greets that person non-verbally.

Sometimes lifting up both eyebrows is supported by lifting up the chin.

This is mostly seen when it is not appropriate to greet somebody verbally (e.g., during a conference, in class, in a meeting).

Both eyebrows are raised for a moment.

2.2.16 Scrunching together eyebrows

The person shows concerns and worry. "I don't really know …"

It also is possible that the person has problems with his work life or with his life in general.

Both eyebrows are pulled together.

2.2.17 Opening the pupils

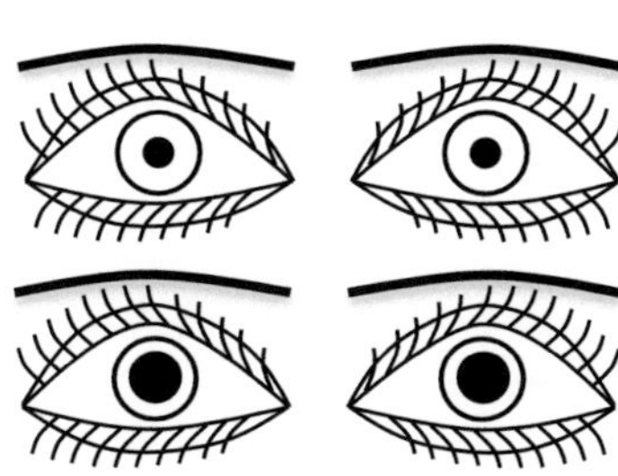

The person likes what he sees a lot. That can be the spoken words or another person.

The other party can interpret this as a positive sign. The person has a positive attitude towards the subject or other person.

Both pupils are opening without change in the light conditions.

2.2.18 Lifting up the eyebrows

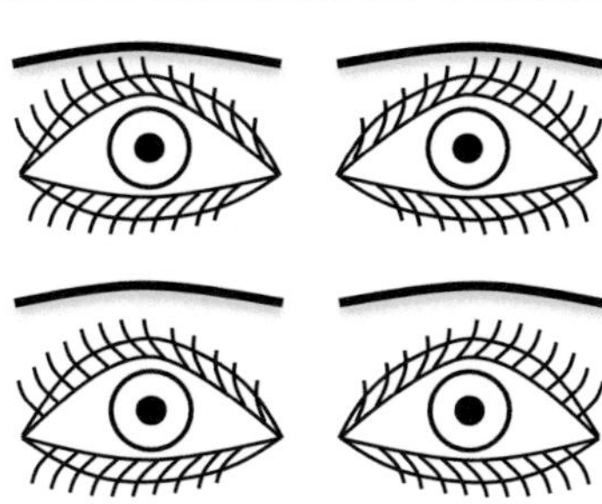

The person demonstrates that he likes a lot what he sees.

You can observe such a gesture when you serve food that taste very good, for example.

This gesture is also seen as an exchange of opinion between two people of the same sex when they agree on seeing an attractive person of the opposite sex.

The eyebrows are lifted up a few times.

2.2.19 Look through some-body

The person is absent-minded.

He wants to demonstrate that he is concentrating and listening but he is actually thinking about something else.

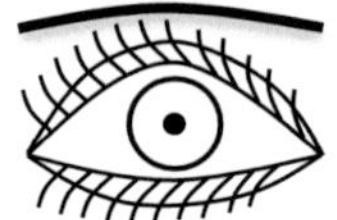

The speaker can get this person to focus by talking directly to him or asking him some questions.

Apparently looking at somebody but actually looking through somebody.

2.2.20 Looking straight at someone

It is possible to have an open ex-change.

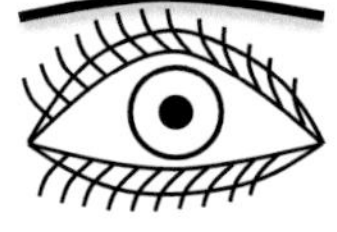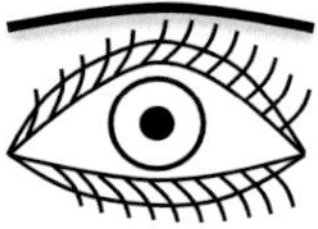

The person looks interested in what the speaker is saying and listens carefully and taking in his explanations and remarks.

This is purely a positive sign for a dialog.

Both eyes are looking directly at the other person.

2.2.21 No eye-contact

The person is uncomfortable and cannot look into the eyes of the other person.

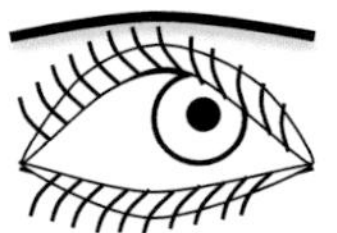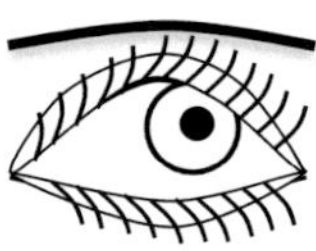

Maybe he is hiding something. In order to have a useful conversa-tion, it is important to create a comfortable and pleasant atmos-phere.

Both eyes are looking past the other person.

2.2.22 Trembling eyelids

Trembling eyelids demonstrate that the person is strained or nervous.

Obviously he does not feel comfortable in the current situation.

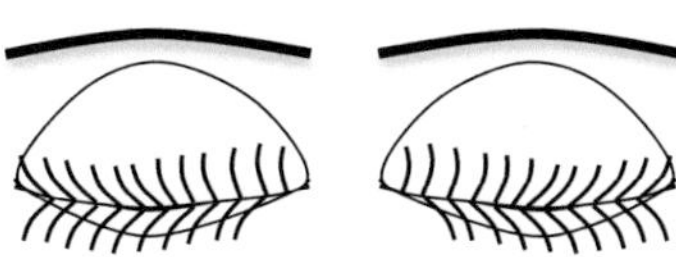

Both eyelids are trembling.

2.2.23 Rubbing eyes

The person is tired, maybe caused through lack of interest or stress.

The counter-party should consider changing the subject or to talking directly to the person.

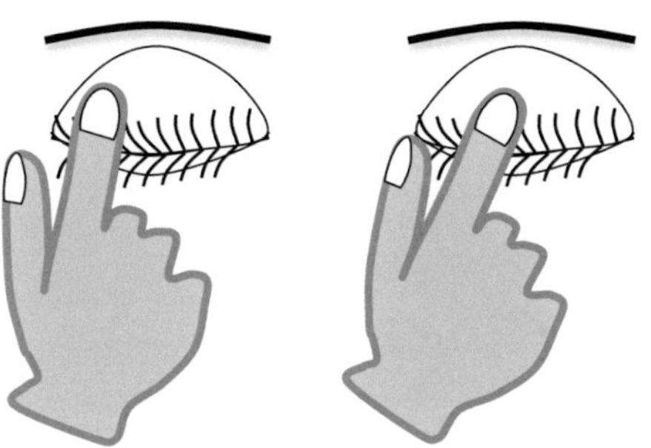

One finger is rubbing the closed eyelid.

59

2.2.24 Wiping the eyes

The person is showing feelings of sadness. "It is so sad, that …"

This gesture is a little bit childish.

The person wants to be cuddled and/or to be consoled.

He is looking for closeness.

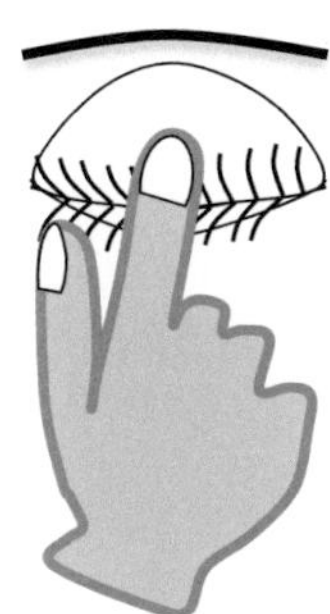

Both eyes are closed.

He is wiping a closed eyelid with one finger.

2.2.25 Pulling down one eyelid

The person demonstrates that he believes that what was said was untrue or that he sees it ironically.

Pulling down one eyelid can be translated with: "You can't play that game with me, you fool!"

One lower eyelid is pulled down with the index finger for a few seconds.

2.2.26 Pushing glasses up the nose

The person is a little bit nervous.

He could start sweating and therefore it is possible that his glasses slide down his nose.

It is also possible that he has something to hide.

The glasses are pushed up the nose with the index finger.

2.2.27 Abruptly taking off glasses

By taking off the glasses, eye-contact with the other person is interrupted for a moment.

That means that the person has something to hide or does not completely tell the truth in this particular situation.

Abruptly taking off the glasses with one hand.

2.2.28 Eye-glasses

The index finger and the thumb
are formed together into a ring
so they mimic binoculars.

The person wants to make the other people understand that somebody from outside is watching them.

The index finger and thumb on each hand are formed together to a
ring. Both rings are hold in front of the eyes.

2.3 Face, cheeks

2.3.1 Abruptly pulling the head back

The distance between two people increases by abruptly pulling back the head.

This increase in distance demonstrates skepticism or suspiciousness toward the other person or what he just said.

The person does not believe or hardly believes what the other person has said.

In a discussion, this kind of gesture demonstrates the rejection of an opinion or despite.

The head is abruptly pulled back.

2.3.2 Tucking the head in between the shoulders

The person wants to make him-self smaller than he actually is. He does not want other people to see him.

To duck one's own head can be interpreted as: "Please, don't hit me, I'm so small."

This gesture indicates anxiety, nervousness, stress, or inner ten-sions.

The shoulders are pressed together and the head is pulled in between the shoulders.

2.3.3 To clutch the nape of the neck

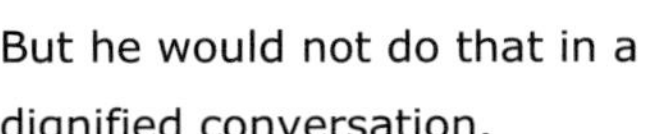

The person lifts his arm because he actually wants to hit the other person.

But he would not do that in a dignified conversation.

Therefore the hand moves to the nape of the neck and clutches tightly. Usually, the head will tip back as well in order to create a little bit pressure.

That demonstrates a certain distance to the other person.

The chest is possibly pushed up as well to demonstrate strength and power. The person absolutely does not agree with the behavior or what the other person just said.

63

To clutch the nape of the neck with one hand from behind.

2.3.4 Massaging the nape of the neck

It strengthens the nape of the neck. The person wants to make himself stronger or he wants to be braver.

He is very nervous and it is advisable to let go of his nervousness.

One should expect some sort of objection from him.

It is also possible that this person is tired due to sitting down too long.

One hand is massaging the nape of the neck.

2.3.5 Stroking the beard

This gesture causes relaxation
and calmness.

He is lost in his thoughts which
do not necessarily relate to the
current subject of the conversation.

One hand slowly strokes the beard or the imaginary beard.

2.3.6 Letting the beard grow

The person demonstrates that he
would grow a long beard himself.

Of course that takes some time.

Unfortunately he does not have the time because the current conversation bores him.

One hand moves down an imaginary long beard.

2.3.7 Twirling the moustache

This gesture brings about calmness and relaxation. He is meditative.

At the same time he is grooming
himself by taking care of his
moustache.

He indicates to the other person that he has a positive attitude towards
him.

Twirling the moustache.

2.3.8 Covering the face

The person is shocked about what he just saw or heard and covers the three main senses: his mouth, i.e., he cannot say anything else; he cannot complain about something or about somebody, he cannot explain his resentment.

His nose – he cannot smell the other person anymore or cannot sense any information about the smell.

His eyes (at least allusively) – he cannot see the other person anymore or does not have to see what is going on.

The hand is put over the face.

The fingers are touching each other and the palm covers the nose and chin.

2.3.9 Swiping an arm across the face

The hand is trying to catch an imaginary mosquito or something else that does not exist.

The gesture demonstrates that a third party lost his mind.

"He lost his mind."

It is seen as a negative gesture because obviously it was not possible to create a corporate atmosphere.

The hand moves with its thumb up across the face.

After that the hand forms a fist to pretend it caught something.

2.3.10 Loosening the collar with one index

Very often this is an easy unconscious manoeuvre. It demonstrates arrogance or pride or
even hidden nervousness.

The speaker should handle the person as an average, completely
normal person.

One index finger moves to the collar and lightly twitches it
to the outside.

2.3.11 Drilling one index finger into the cheek

The index finger does not move
to the temple, but for "safety"
reasons and drills a little bit
lower into the cheek. This gesture indicates the opinion:
"You're crazy!"

The index finger touches the middle of the cheek and twists
around several times.

2.3.12 Lightly hit the cheek

"How stupid am I?" is what this
gesture means.

The little tap on the cheek
demonstrates a small punish-
ment to himself.

A little tap with the fingers of an outstretched hand on
one's own cheek.

2.3.13 Hitting oneself on the head

"Oops, how could I be so dumb?" Or: "I could punish myself for what I just did."

The person realized that he did something or said something he should not have done or said; at least from his own point of view.

Lightly hitting the head with one open hand.

2.3.14 Smirking with the corner of the mouth

This is a gesture of sarcasm. Obviously some sort of smile.

In reality this demonstrates arrogance or conte.

One corner of the mouth is slightly raised up.

2.3.15 Puffing up cheeks

One puffed up cheek indicates:

"Uh, what are you talking about …?"

Two puffed up cheeks indicate:

"That is huge …" Or: "Uh, I can't eat anymore. I'm full."

Oder: „Puh, ich kann nicht mehr. Ich bin satt."

One or two puffed up cheeks.

2.3.16 Scratching the head

The person is nervous and
maybe he just got caught saying
or doing something that is not
100 % correct or appropriate.

The arm is lifted for protection (maybe to indicate that he is ready to
defend himself); then the arm moves to the head and starts scratching the scalp.

Scratching the head with one hand.

2.3.17 Gently shaking the head

"Well, whatever you just said –
I'm not so sure about it. I'm
skeptical."

The person does not agree with the explanations and statements and
mentions his concerns.

The head gently shakes from the left to the right.

2.3.18 Nodding the head

The person demonstrates
through nodding the head that
he completely agrees.

This kind of gesture is important for a positive conversation.

The speaker can quickly loose his nervousness at the beginning of a
speech because of gestures like that from the audience.

Nodding the head once or several times.

2.3.19 Pulling the head back

Pulling the head up and back establishes distance from the other person.

That demonstrates that the person does not agree with what was just said.

Very often the eyes will be open widely as well which also shows a surprise. In an extreme case it can mean: "I can't believe what I just figured out/realized!"

The head is pulled back.

2.3.20 Scratching the neck

The person is a little bit nervous.

He cannot clarify what he just heard. "I'm not sure …"

Scratching the neck or right underneath the ear with one finger.

2.3.21 To beckon somebody with the head

The head moves in one direction. It is possible that the person cannot use his arms at the moment to indicate a certain direction.

This gesture can be interpreted as follows: "Come here." Or: "Let's go this direction."

Pointing or nodding the head once or several times in a certain direction.

2.3.22 Touching the part of the hair

"Oops, how could I be so dumb?"

The person touches slightly his head and indicates that he just said something unwise.

The open hand is laid on the part of the hair.

2.3.23 Moving the hands through the hair

This gesture shows that the person is pensive.

Like twirling the moustache the person is grooming himself by talking care of his hair and he wants to indicate the other person that he has a positive attitude towards him.

Scratching the neck or right underneath the ear with one finger.

2.3.24 Shaking one's head

The person demonstrates his objection, disfavour, and antipathy clearly: "No, no, no …"

He absolutely does not agree with what just said or happened.

If the eyes look down to the ground as the person shakes his head they are talking about a third person.

"I can't believe how he/she could ever do that."

The head shakes several times from the right to the left side.

2.3.25 Leaning on the left cheek

The person listens attentively to the conversation and tries to process the information objectively, logically, and critically (left brain hemisphere).

For right-handed people.

For left-handed people see the gesture described in 2.3.26.

The left cheek leans on one hand.

The head moves a little bit to the left.

2.3.26 Leaning on the right cheek

71

The person listens attentively to the conversation and tries to process the information objectively, logically, and critically (right brain hemisphere).

For left-handed people.

For right-handed people see the gesture described in 2.3.25.

The right cheek leans on one hand.

The head moves a little bit to the right.

2.3.27 Leaning the head on one's fist

There are two possible interpretations: One – the person is listening closely and concentrating, or two – the person is completely bored.

The head is leaning on one fist.

Sometimes the index finger spreads away from the hand and leans on the cheek.

2.3.28 Laying the head down on folded hands

There are two possible interpretations: One – the person is listening closely and concentrating, or two – the person is tired and the head is so heavy that he needs to hold it up with his hands.

The chin is leaning on the hands which are folded together.

2.4 Chin

2.4.1 Stroking one's chin

The person is meditative or pensive but he is also listening to the explanations and remarks.

He is content and just feels fine.

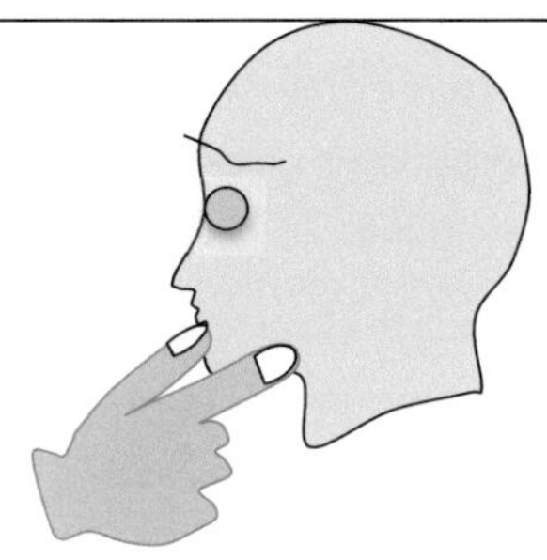

Thumb and index finger are stroking the chin.

2.4.2 Bracing the chin

The person is forcing himself to pay attention. "Well, I think I will listen to this very closely."

It is expected that the person may object to the discussion.

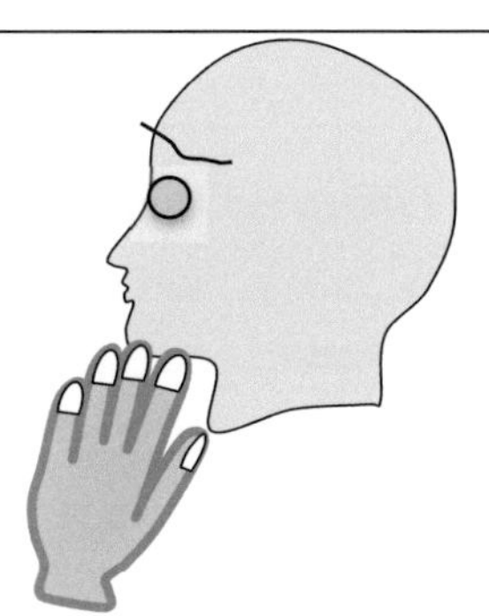

The chin is braced with four fingers touching each other.

2.4.3 Laying the chin on the index finger

The person is attentive: "Nobody can fool me."

He is skeptical towards the explanations and remarks of the speaker and he pays attention to everything that is said and done. He will object whenever he determines there is an inaccuracy or weakness in the speaker.

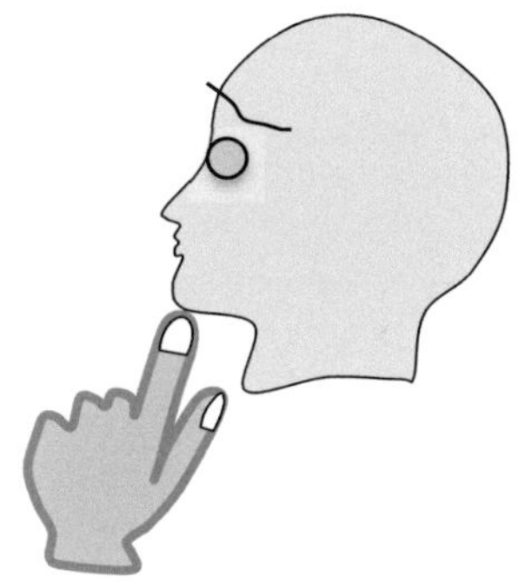

The chin lies on top of the tip of the index finger.

2.4.4 Pointing with chin

The person points with his
chin to another person or to
another thing.

This is not the friendliest
gesture because it is mostly
used to point at somebody
when it is not wanted that
the person realizes it.

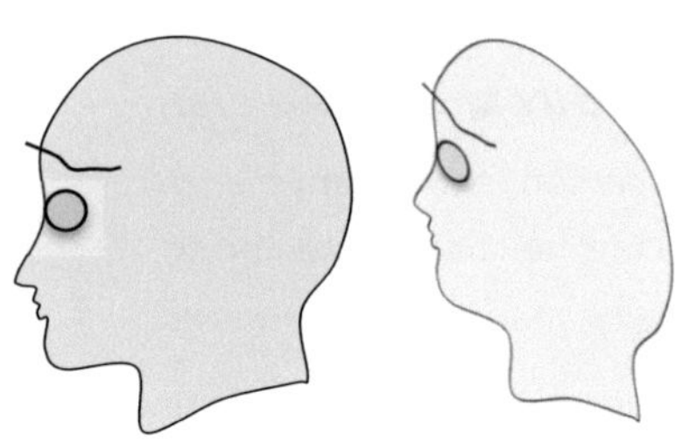

Pointing with the chin in a certain direction.

2.4.5 Lifting up the chin

When the chin is lifted up along
with the head.

That means the person is raising
himself above all people who are
present.

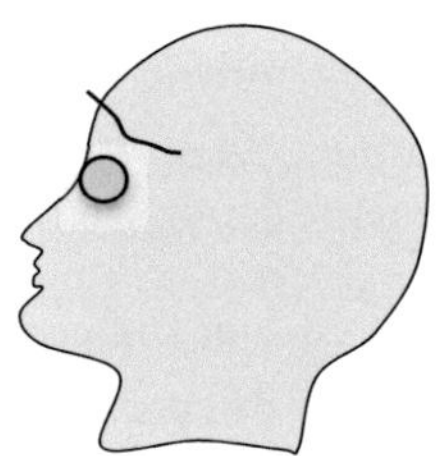

Verbally this could be formulated as follows: "I'm not interested in all
that!"

Or: "Well, see if you can reach an agreement!"

Or: "Without me!"

The person excludes himself from a group.

The chin is lifted up.

2.4.6 Flipping a finger off the chin

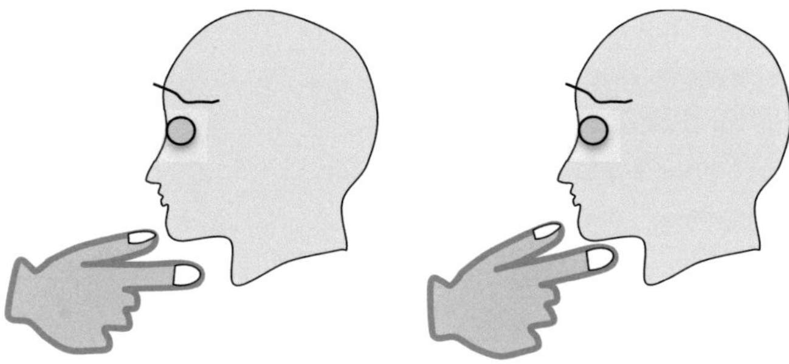

"You can't fool me!"

This is how the gesture is translated best.

The index finger or several fingers of one hand are flipping in front and along the chin. The movement goes from the neck to the chin.

2.4.7 Knocking underneath at the chin

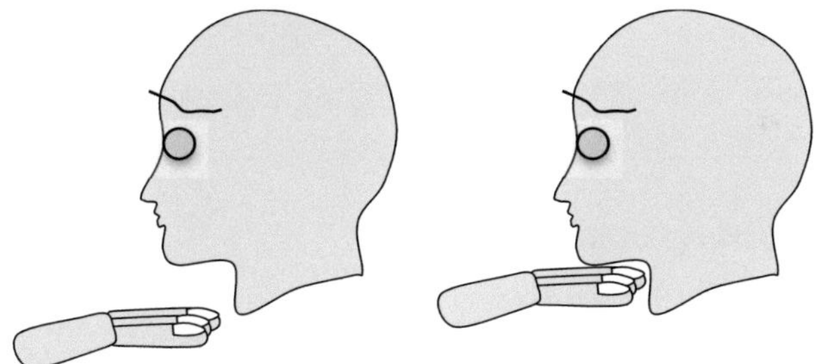

Visually the person demonstrates he is in deep water.

"It's standing up here!"

He does not agree anymore with what is going on.

From this point on it is expected that the person objects.

The flat hand with spread-eagled fingers knocks one time or several times from underneath at the chin.

2.4.8 Scratching the chin

The person is not sure whether he agrees with the argumentation and concept of the speaker or to the opinions and judgments of the audience.

This gesture demonstrates the inconclusiveness of the person.

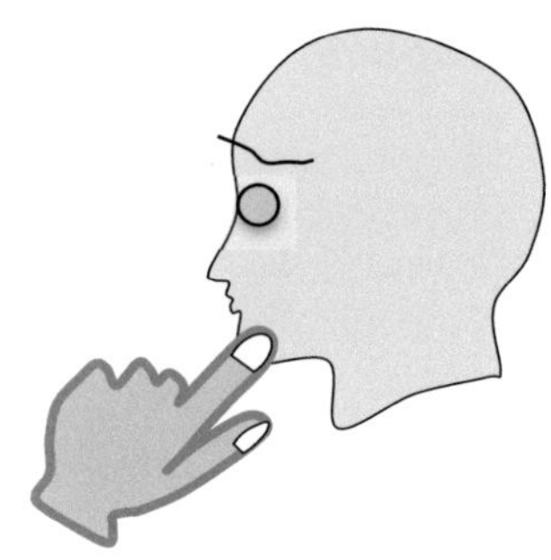

One or several fingers are scratching the chin.

2.4.9 Massaging the chin with the whole hand

The person demonstrates skepticism and incredulousness.

"I can't believe what you just said!"

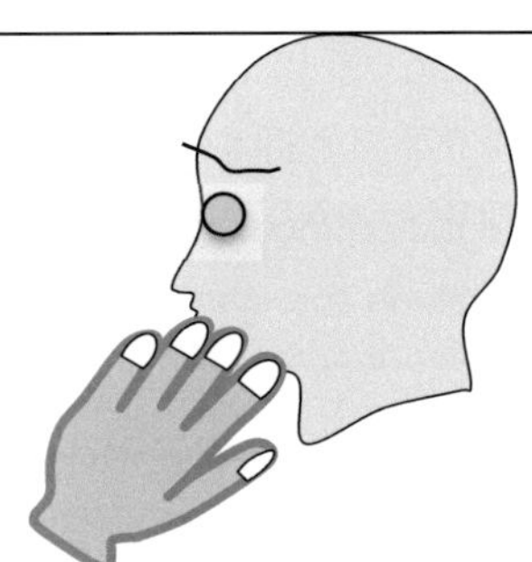

Massaging the chin with the whole hand.

2.4.10 Sticking out the chin

The gesture demonstrates aggression:

"What do you want from me?"

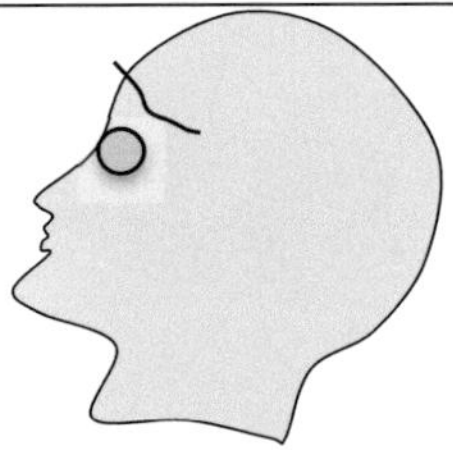

The chin is clearly sticking out.

2.4.11 Pulling the chin in

The person makes himself smaller and backs off.

The gesture demonstrates fear, restraint, and constraint.

The head is pulled down and therefore the eyes look down to the floor.

It definitely is a gesture of extreme humility.

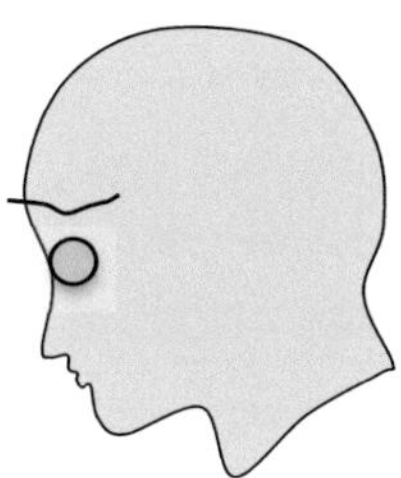

The chin is pulled in.

2.5 Nose

2.5.1 Touching the nose

The position of the fingers covers part of the mouth and the nostril's; obviously the person wants to hide something.

Candour and openness can be created if applicable through an atmosphere free of fear.

The index finger of one hand presses from underneath on the nose.

It may be underneath the nostril or next to the nose pointing to one eye.

2.5.2 Holding one's nose

It is a gesture that is easy to analyze: "I can't stand you!"

Obviously the person does not like the other person.

It also is possible that it just smells unpleasant and a verbal explanation follows.

Both nostrils are closed with thumb and index finger.

2.5.3 Pushing up the nose

The person is forcing himself to get along with the other person. He is not sure at all if the events are fitting in with his personal preferences.

"I'm not really sure at the moment."

Or: "I have to think about it."

Very often the person can be convinced.

The index finger is used to push-up the tip of the nose.

2.5.4 Sticking the nose up

When the nose is lifted up the head goes up as well. The person's head is above other people who are present and wants to demonstrate that he thinks that he is superior.

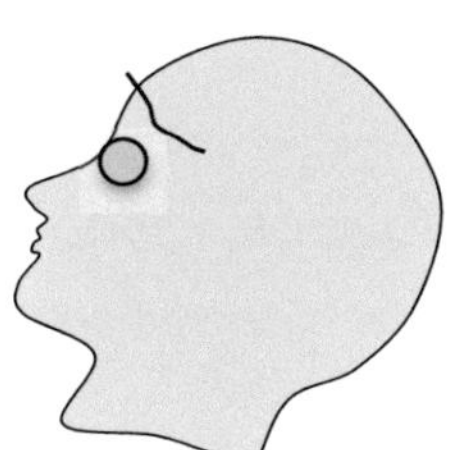

Therefore, a gesture like that is interpreted as being stuck-up or snobbish.

Verbally this could be formulated as follows: "I'm not interested in all that!"

Or: "Well, see if you can reach an agreement!"

Or: "Without me!"

The person excludes himself knowingly from a group.

The nose is held up intensively.

2.5.5 Tapping the nose

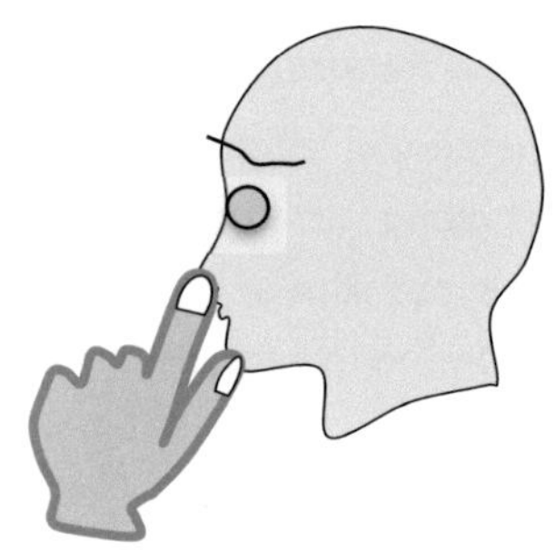

The person suddenly has a thought: "I just got an idea!"

Generally, there has been a lot of consideration about this idea.

It is expected that this idea is creative and constructive.

To tap on one side of the nose once or several times.

2.5.6 Wrinkling the nose

This gesture demonstrates pretty clearly that the person cannot or does not want to smell something. "Ugh, I don't like that!"

It demonstrates disgust, nausea, or dislike.

The nose is pulled up and wrinkled.

2.5.7 To cook a snook

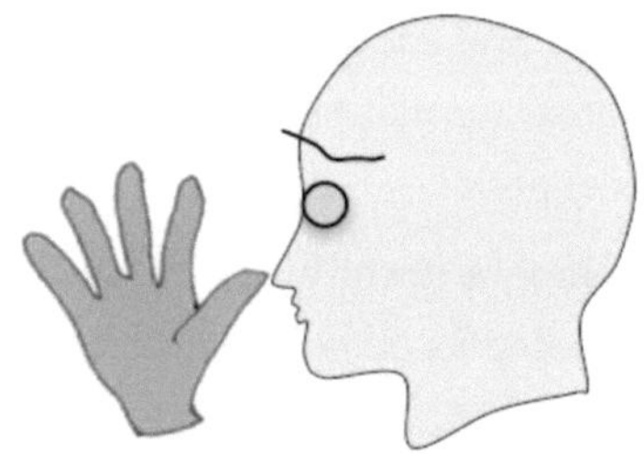

The nose is extended artificially.

The person makes a funny comment on slightly wrong behavior, mistake, or failure of another person or group.

It is also possible to use this gesture if the respective person or group won or got an advantage in a game: "Ha, ha, ha!"

The thumb touches the tip of the nose.

The other fingers are spread out and wiggle.

2.5.8 Wrinkling the nose to the side

The nose is taken out of the direction where certain information comes from (e.g., a possible smell).

Visually, the person does not want to or have to see or smell the other person at the moment.

He is showing disapproval toward the other person.

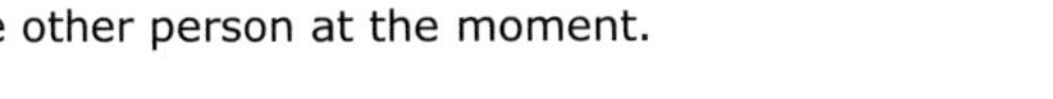

The tip of the nose is quickly pressed to the side.

2.5.9 Breathing deeply through the nostrils

The person is taking a deep breath to prepare of for attack.

 He is really mad.

It is absolutely expected to get an aggressive objection or even a verbal attack.

Both nostrils are blown up

81

2.5.10 Flaring nostrils

The person is really mad and angry inside.

But he feels his inferiority.

Both nostrils of the nose start to rise. It is possible that the person begins to cry.

The nostrils are raising or fluttering.

2.6 Forehead, temple, ear

2.6.1 Tapping in the middle of one's forehead

This gesture means: "You have bats in your belfry!"

The index finger is used to tap in the middle of the forehead.

2.6.2 Tapping on the side of one's forehead

Do not mistake this gesture with the gesture in 2.6.1.

This gesture means something completely different. "Hmm, that's clever!"

The person admires a third person or looks up to that person.

It is also used when a person got a brilliant idea: "Yes, that is a really good idea!"

The index finger is used to tap on the side of the forehead.

83

2.6.3 Tapping on one's forehead with all fingers

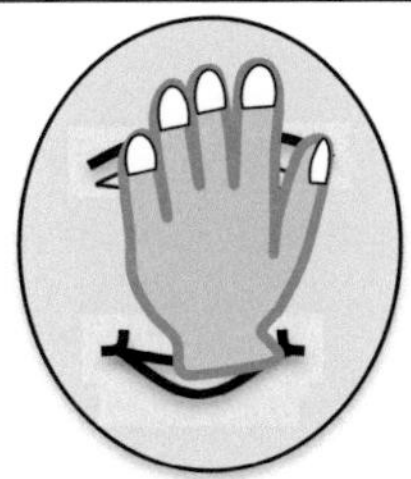

Here the person calls somebody else crazy.

All fingers of one hand tap on the front of the forehead.

2.6.4 Pressing on the fore-head

The person indicates that he is not feeling well.

Generally, the eyes are closed when this gesture is seen.

This gesture also means: "I can't believe what you just said."

"I really get sick when I hear that!"

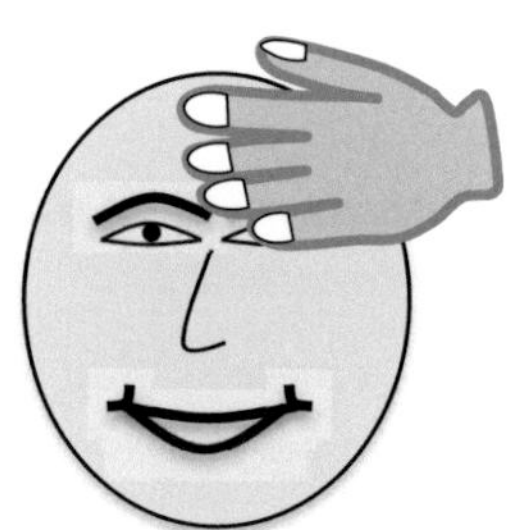

Pressing with all fingers of one hand on the forehead.

2.6.5 Hitting the forehead with an open hand

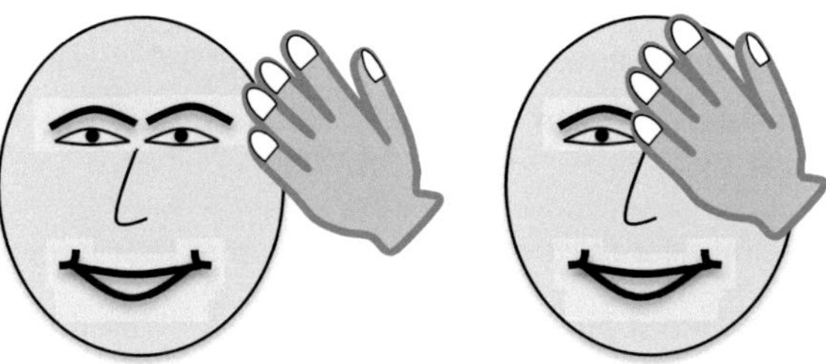

"Man, am I dumb! Why didn't I get it in the first place?"

With this gesture the person calls himself stupid.

The person already realized that there is a better solution and there-fore this gesture is seen positively.

Lightly hit the forehead with on open hand.

2.6.6 Wiping one's forehead

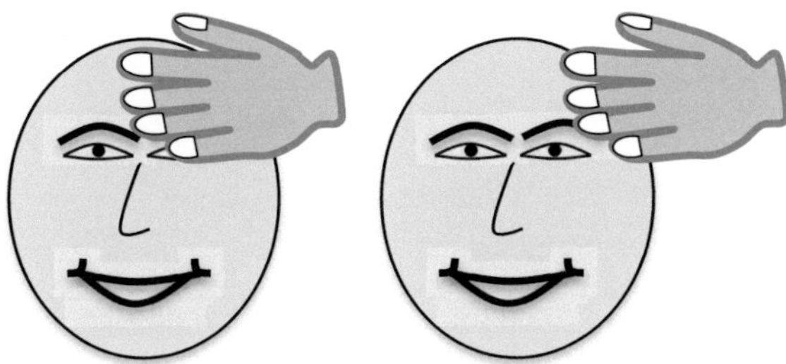

Symbolically the person is wiping sweat off his forehead because he just managed a dicey situation.

The gesture can be translated with: "I got lucky!"

Wiping the hand over the forehead.

2.6.7 Knocking on the forehead

It is sometimes difficult to force others to internalize or accept others thoughts or ideas.

Therefore stubborn people are sometimes called "bullhead".
"He's not getting it!"

Usually this gesture is used when talking about a third person.

Knocking on the forehead with the knuckles of a fist.

2.6.8 Drilling in one's temple

This gesture means that one person is called crazy.

This is not a positive gesture and it is highly recommended to have a talk to clear up the situation.

The index finger drills a hole into the temple.

2.6.9 Twirling a finger in a small circle at the temple

This gesture also should demonstrate that a third person is "not completely normal in his head."

As long as this gesture is used as a joke it is generally acceptable.

The index finger of one hand is circling around the temple.

2.6.10 Shooting in one's temple

Symbolically the person shots himself in his temple.

This gesture demonstrates that the person made a huge mistake or was foolish.

Therefore he should actually kill himself.

This gesture is <u>only</u> intended as a joke!

The index and middle finger are touching the temple.

The thumb is extended and the ring and pinky finger are bent together.

2.6.11 Knit one's brow

The person is demonstrating skepticism.

He is not completely sure if he correctly heard or saw something.

"Hmm, is that really right?"

The forehead wrinkles.

2.6.12 Covering the ears with the hands

There are two different inter-

pretations for this gesture:

One – it is too loud for the per-

son and two – he does not

want to listen to somebody

else: "I don't want to hear

what you have to say!"

The ears are covered by using both hands.

2.6.13 Pushing the ear forward

The person changes the angle of

his ear for sound waves so that

he can better catch sound waves

and hear better.

The speaker should speak up or eliminate disturbing sounds.

One hand is pressing the ear forward from behind.

2.6.14 Enlarging one's ear

Artificially, the person enlarges his ear to better understand what other people are talking about.

The speaker should talk louder or eliminate disturbing sounds.

The gesture can also been used when the person acoustically understood what the speaker said but still want to interfere: "What did you just say?"

"I think I didn't understand you right."

One hand is behind the ear.

The thumb is lying on the head in front of the ear.

The open hand is seen by the other person.

2.6.15 Make a donkey ear

The gesture symbolizes the ears of a donkey and is shown to the other person.

It demonstrates what the person thinks about the other one.

"You're an [old] donkey!"

This is not a serious gesture and is used to be funny or as a joke.

The thumb touches the ear and the other fingers are spread widely.

2.6.16 Putting fingers in one's ears

The gesture is similar to picture 2.6.12 (*Covering the ears with the hands*) where the ears are covered entirely with the hands.

The interpretation is pretty much the same:

1. The speaker is too loud. The level of extraneous noise should be decreased.

2. The person does not want to accept another opinion.

The index fingers of both hands are put into the ears.

2.6.17 Playing with one's earlobe

The person is nervous and restrained at the moment.

He wants to be cuddled and loved.

Nobody is doing that at the moment and therefore he is lost in thoughts playing with his earlobe.

Thumb and index finger are playing with the earlobe.

2.6.18 Flipping the ear from behind

"Hmm, I don't think that I heard what you just said correctly.

You naughty little devil …"

It is a funny little gesture when the speaker just used ambiguous words.

The index finger flips the ear once or several times to the front.

2.6.19 Pinching one's earlobe

The person wants to "drag the other person along."

He cannot really do that and therefore he pinches his own earlobe instead.

The thumb and index finger are used to pinch the earlobe.

2.6.20 Scratching one's ear

The person demonstrates nervousness and uncertainty.

The index finger is scratching the ear.

2.6.21 2.6.12 Scratching behind one's ear

The person is nervous and not confident.

He cannot really understand what he heard.

"I do not really know ..."

One finger (generally the index finger) is scratching behind the ear.

Chapter 3

93

Unlocking the secrets of body language: The body

3.1 Upper part of the body, shoulder, chest, stomach

3.1.1 Deeply bending the upper part of the body

The distance between two people decreases significantly by using this posture.

The difference from the posture in 3.1.2 is that this posture invades into the personal space of the other person and he might get uncomfortable (i.e., negative posture).

This posture demonstrates arrogance or presumptuousness and creates negative or aggressive feelings.

The upper part of the body is deeply bent over towards the other person (invading his personal space).

3.1.2 Bending over the upper part of the body

The distance between two people decreases by using this posture.

Both people want to be closer in order to better connect to each other

This posture is positive for the person because it indicates that the other person is interested in what he is talking about.

It is expected to have a valuable co-operation for both sides.

The upper part of the body is bent over towards the other person.

3.1.3 Leaning back the upper part of the body

The distance between two people increases by using this posture.

That means that there is no sign of agreement and the individuals do not want to get close to each other.

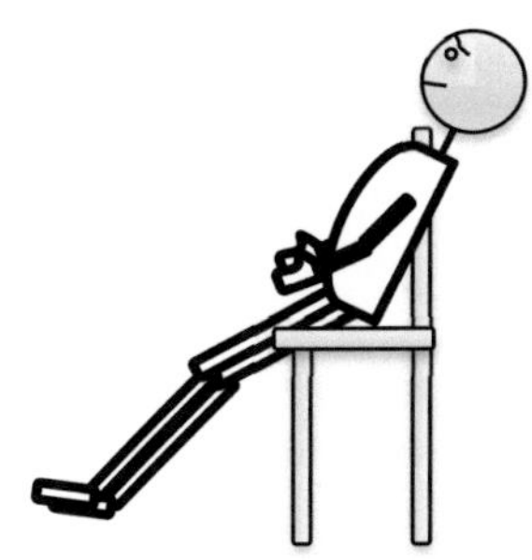

95

This is critical because there is obvious disfavor about the subject or the latest statement.

The upper part of the body is leaned back and far away from the other person.

3.1.4 Bowing one's body to the front

This posture demonstrates that the person is attentively listening.

If the head is tucked down as well, it is a posture of humility.

Standing up or sitting down, the upper part of the body is bowed towards the other person.

3.1.5 Hunching shoulders

The person makes himself smaller and protects himself by hunching his shoulders tightly together.

Generally, this posture is seen together with the head turning down.

This posture is usually evaluated as being negative because it symbolizes constraint and shyness.

The shoulders are hunched tightly together leaning to the front.

3.1.6 Give someone a pat on the back

This gesture may be seen as an invasion of one's personal space but it is meant as a gesture of friendship and it symbolizes closeness and empathy.

It also can be used to encourage somebody.

This gesture is usually used in a positive atmosphere but the person using it should make sure that the other person is comfortable with this gesture.

To give the other person a pat on the back.

3.1.7 Shrugging shoulders

A statement that is easy to understand: "I don't know."

Or: "I can't imagine what was just said."

It is possible that this kind of statement comes together with a certain level of disinterest towards the subject.

Shrugging the shoulders once or several times.

3.1.8 Linking one's arms underneath the armpits

A person who behaves like that is satisfied with himself and his environment and is open towards everything.

This gesture can be seen as arrogant or presumptuous by others

The thumbs are linked underneath the armpits and the other fingers are fan-shaped and widespread.

3.1.9 Cutting a hand at the level of the stomach

"I have had it up to here!"

The person is "fed up" Or: "Has had it!"

With this gesture he wants to demonstrate that he wants to be cut off from the subject.

The flat hand makes a cutting gesture in front of his stomach from the left to the right side. The palm of the hand is down.

3.1.10 Tapping on the stomach

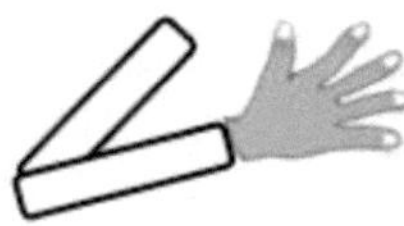

The attention is directed to the well-fed stomach. It is a sign the person is feeling fine and is well-fed.

Together with this posture, often the upper part of the body leans back.

Tapping lightly on the stomach with one or both hands.

3.1.11 Holding one's hand on the stomach

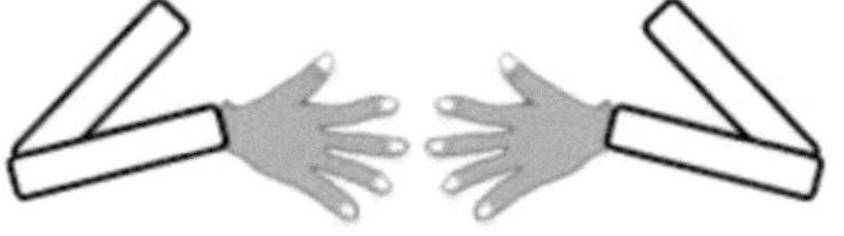

"I'm happy and satisfied. I have had enough to eat."

Sometimes it is a sign that the person ate too much and feels overly full.

This posture is seen often after lunch break.

The physical energy went from the head to the stomach to digest the food.

Therefore, "brain work" is barely possible.

One or two hands are lying on the stomach.

3.1.12 Tapping the chest (1)

The index finger points on the chest and the person asks the other person: "Are you talking to me?"

Very often it goes together with knitting one's brow (see 2.6.8: *Knit one's brow*).

This posture is often seen if somebody is accused of something bad that happened for no good reason.

Generally the person is in a good mood and it is easy to clear up the situation.

Tapping with the index finger on the chest.

The index finger stays there for a few seconds.

3.1.13 Tapping the chest (2)

The person wants to call attention to himself. "Hello, I'm still
here. This means me."

Sometimes it is also used educa-
tional to support the verbal statement: "I've always told you ..."

The index finger taps several times on the chest.

3.1.14 Pressing on the chest

This is a slightly aggressive posture.

"I have to hold myself back! Otherwise I'll explode!"

The person is angry or furious at
a person he wants to attack but
the person is usually not present.

By holding the fists close to his own body the person tries to hold
himself back.

This kind of posture is supported to correlative facial expressions.

One or two fist are clenched together and pressed against the chest..

3.1.15 Holding the chest

This posture demonstrates a complete surprise. The person feels verbally attacked and asserts his innocence surprise. "I am not aware of being accused of anything."

Usually the eyebrows are lifted up in surprise.

One or both hands are lying on the chest and they press a little bit on the chest.

3.1.16 Knocking on the chest

The person wants to get the attention of the other people. "Hello, I'm still here. This means me."

This gesture is mostly used to support verbal expressions.

The closed fingertips of one or both hands are knocking a few times on the chest.

3.1.17 Beating on the chest

This is a body movement that is normally seen with men. It demonstrates how strong and powerful the person is. It is possible to compare this gesture with the fauna (e.g., specific species of monkeys).

Very often this gesture is used to be funny or as a joke.

One or both fists are beating several times on the chest.

3.1.18 Crossing one's arms in front of the chest

With this posture the person protests his innocence.

"I wash my hands of it. I swear!"

This posture is in Islamic cultures also seen as greeting.

The hands and arms lay crossed on the chest.

3.1.19 Laying both arms in front of the stomach

This is a weaker form of the posture "Folding one's arms in front of the upper part of the body" (see 4.1.1: *Folding one's arms in front of the upper part of the body*).

This posture demonstrates that the person is insecure and constrained and that he holds on tightly to himself.

He wants to protect his body from possible attack.

Both arms are parallel to each other and held in front of his stomach.

3.1.20 Laying the left hand on the chest

This is a protest of innocence.

"I swear!"

Or: "On my honor ..."

The person demonstrates that he has nothing to hide.

One hand lies on the chest. Usually it is the left hand.

3.1.21 Opening one's jacket during a conversation

There are two possibilities for an interpretation of this gesture:

1. "It is too warm for me. I don't feel that good in my skin. I'd like to shed my skin."

2. It could be a certain form of arrogance.

The person demonstrates to the other person that he is superior to him and that he can decide by himself to open his jacket informally in a formal conversation.

The buttons of the jacket will be opened during a formal conversation.

3.1.22 Arms folded behind the back

To hide the arms from other people demonstrates nervousness and constraint.

The person tries to hold on to himself, so to speak.

If the hands and arms are hidden behind the back, the other person cannot interpret anything from the posture of the arms and hands because he cannot see them.

For self-conscious people this is a good possibility to step up or to speak relaxed in front of a group.

One hand is holding the other arm behind the back.

3.1.23 Laying an arm behind the back

If one arm is behind the back the person is slightly embarrassed about something.

The other person cannot see what the hand is doing behind the back.

One arm is laying behind the back at the height of the kidneys.

Chapter 4

105

Unlocking the secrets of body language: The arms

4.1 Elbow/arms

4.1.1 Folding one's arms in front of the upper part of the body

This posture is a reaction to something that has just happened and it is viewed negatively.

106

The person closes himself and maybe is afraid, constrained, or he feels uncomfortable.

Therefore out of fear he tries to protect himself.

As long as the person has this posture, he blocks everything and is not able to or does not want to gather or accept new arguments or information.

The other person should try to release the tense situation because the person is not able to participate in a normal conversation before he moves down his arms.

Both arms are crossed in front of the chest.

One hand can be seen and the other one is hidden behind one arm.

4.1.2 Striking out one's arm

The person strikes his arm straight out to one side during his speech or presentation.

This motion demonstrates enormous self-confidence.

The person is not afraid to open up to others.

Striking out one arm as the person gesticulates.

4.1.3 Confined arm movement

The person barely moves his arms away from his body during his speech or presentation.

To gesticulate like that demonstrates a little bit of uncertainty or insecurity.

The arm is always close to the body and is ready to quickly protect the person if necessary.

Confined arm movement as the person gesticulates.

4.1.4 Holding up both arms

Usually this posture can be seen positively.

"Look, I'm great!" Or: "Great, I won again!"

The person demonstrates enthusiasm and a positive attitude.

The hands build a fist and both arms are held up until they are a little bit above the head.

4.1.5 Holding up both arms above the head

This posture demonstrates enormous enthusiasm: "Wonderful, we won, we are the champions!"

It is a much stronger posture than seen in picture 4.1.5 and it is only used in situations when it relieves pressure or stress.

Usually it is seen positively.

The hands build fists and both arms are held up way above the head.

The fists may move around quickly and in a hectic manner.

4.1.6 Both arms hanging down informally on the side of the body

This is a relaxing, neutral, and open posture.

It demonstrates that the person is open towards his other person and open for new information.

Both arms are hanging down informally or casual on the side of the body.

4.1.7 Laying the arms behind the head

Usually the upper part of the body is lying back as well when a person has his arms behind his head.

This posture demonstrates that the person tries to relax and drifts out of the situation a little bit.

Maybe the other person should suggest having a break.

Both arms are lying behind the head.

4.1.8 Raising an arm

This gesture is to attract attention.

"Hello, here I am!"

One arm is raised way above the head.

The speaker should see his palm of the hand.

Shaking one hand and grasping the other arm

When two people shake hands it is an invasion in the personal space if one person grasps the other person's arm at the same time.

If they have an on-going and mutual relationship with each other, only the superior would grasp the arm.

It is a relatively positive gesture and should create a relaxed atmosphere.

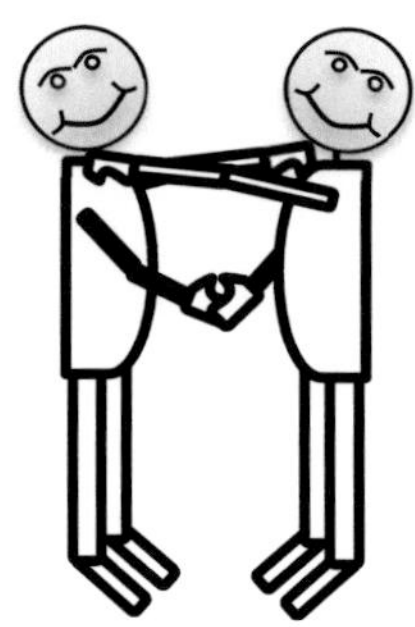

The lefts hand grasps the forearm of the other person while they are shaking hands.

4.1.10 Stretching out one's arms

The person shortens the distance to the other person by stretching out his arms towards him.

This posture is seen positively.

It also means: "Welcome!"

Or: "Come here."

Both arms are stretched into the direction of the other person.

The thumbs point up.

4.1.11 Holding the arms behind the back

There are two possible explanations:

1. "I feel fine." The front side of the body faces open towards the other person.

No confrontation is expected because it would take too much time to bring the hands up front to protect himself.

2. "I'm a little bit nervous."

The person hides his hands behind his back so that the other person cannot see them twitching.

Both arms are held behind the back.

There the wrists are crossing each other.

One hand holds the other wrist.

4.1.12 Holding arms to the hips

Through this gesture the person wants to artificially make himself bigger than he really is.

This posture can be translated as: "Stay away or you're in trouble!"

For whatever reason, the person is aggressive. The other person should try to release the existing tension or aggression.

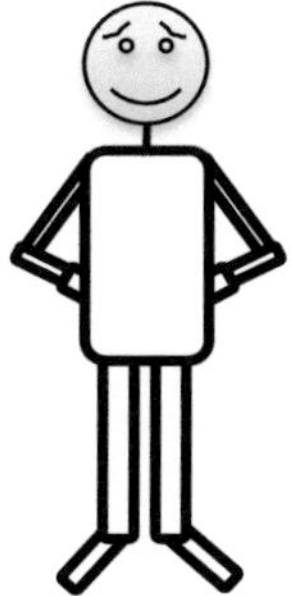

Both arms are held to the hips.

4.1.13 Flexing arm muscles

The person wants to demonstrate how strong and powerful he is.

This gesture is usually meant to be funny or as a joke.

The arm is lifted up and the arm muscles are flexed.

4.1.14 Both arms lying underneath the table

Obviously the person is not feeling well in the current situation.

Maybe he is nervous, constrained, or stressed.

He is hiding both arms underneath the desk top so that the other person cannot see his cramped fingers and his inner tension.

Both arms are lying on the thighs underneath the desk top.

4.1.15 Forearms lying on the table

The person's arms are not forming a barrier because they are open.

That demonstrates an open posture but is also possible to close them quickly if needed.

The person is attentive and has nothing to hide.

This posture can be seen positively.

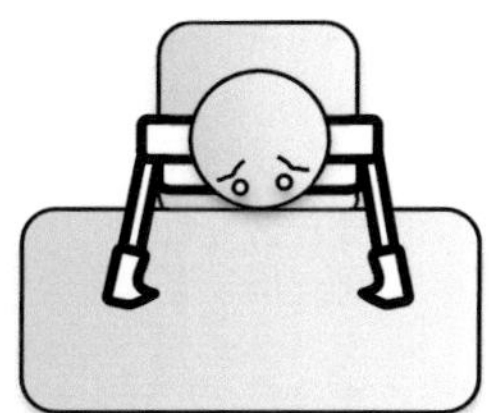

Both forearms are lying parallel to each other on the table.

The hands are lying on the edge and fingers pointing into the direction of the other person.

4.1.16 Propping one's head on a fist

The head is getting so heavy that it needs to be held up.

Maybe he is tired?

The person is generally interested in the subject because this way his head is closer to the other person.

The elbow lies on the table and the chin is propped on top of the fist.

4.1.17 Lying both forearms on the table

On the one hand the person is interested in what is going on and on the other hand he wants to protect himself.

The arms establish a barrier.

The other person should try to create a stress-free and fearless situation or atmosphere.

If he successfully does that, the person will take his arms away and will be open to the information and to the other person.

Both forearms are lying parallel to each other on the table.

4.1.18 Lying one forearm on the table and the other one underneath the table

The person is searching for a contact. The arm lying on the table demonstrates that. But the person is also constrained and shy.

The other person should try to establish a stress-free and fearless situation or atmosphere.

If he successfully does that the person will take his arms away and will be open to the information and to the other person.

One forearm is lying on the table and the other one is underneath the table.

4.1.19 A forearm lying bent on the table

The person orientates himself towards the other person at the table.

The arm lying on the table creates a barrier from the other person.

Nobody should interrupt their conversation at this specific moment.

The forearm which is further away from the other person is lying on the table.

The other forearm is lying on the table as well directly against the body at the height of his stomach.

115

4.1.20 A forearm lying in between the other person

The arm lying in between the two people sitting at a table demonstrates that a barrier is built up in between them.

The person does not really want to have personal contact with his neighbor.

In order to strengthen this posture it is possible that the person also turns his upper part of the body around a little bit showing his neighbor a little bit of his back.

The forearm which is closer to the neighbor is lying on the table and is bent.

The other forearm is lying on the table as well directly next to the body at the height of his stomach.

4.2 Hands, fist

4.2.1 Hands latch on to the sides of a chair

The person is nervous and un-settled.

He is trying to hide his stress by latching his hands onto the chair.

This way the other person can-not see his hands which might reveal his stress.

The other person should try to relax the situation in order to create a positive atmosphere.

The person is latching his hands onto the chair which he is sitting on.

4.2.2 Hitting with an open hand on the table

The person wants to emphasize what he just said. "That's it! That's the way we do it!"

If the person leans back in his chair after this statement than it is a clear sign that the case is decided and the decision is final.

Hitting with an open hand on the table.

4.2.3 Hands held on the hips

Through this gesture the person wants to make himself stronger and bigger than he actually is.

On one hand this posture is a sign of a "show off" or display and on the other hand it can demonstrate outrage:

"Well, let me tell you some-thing!"

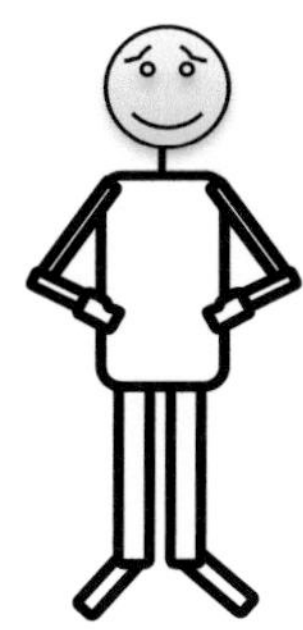

Both hands are held on the hips.

4.2.4 One hand tucked in a pocket

It should be a sign of being re-laxed. Possibly the person is hid-ing a slight uncertainty.

Even if this posture is generally accepted in today's business so-ciety it should not be used in the first few minutes of a conversa-tion.

The person wants to demon-strate that he is feeling relaxed and secure.

Actually he is hiding the hand which could tell a lot about his real feelings.

One hand is tucked into the trousers pocket.

4.2.5 Both hands tucked in trouser pockets

In today's business environment, this posture is generally seen as impolite and arrogant.

The person wants to demonstrate that he controls the situation.

The truth actually is that the person is most likely nervous.

The other person could hand this person some sort of document so that he has to take at least one hand out of his trouser pocket.

Therefore the person can hold onto the document.

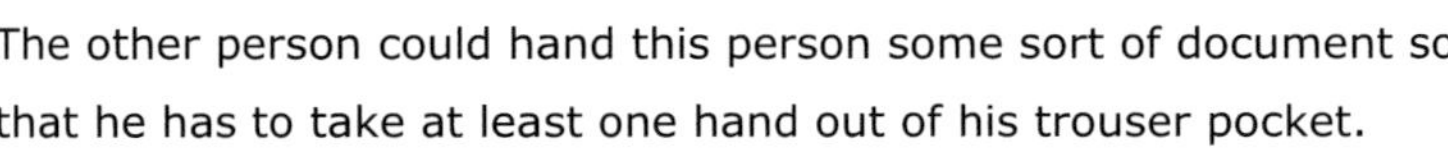

Both hands are put into the trouser pockets.

4.2.6 Form a pitched roof with the hands

To symbolize a pitch roof, the fingers of both hands touch each other and the fingertips pointing upward.

This gesture demonstrates arrogance. "Well, now you listen to me."

If the fingertips point to the other person, a confrontation can be expected.

The fingertips of both hands are touching and they are forming a pitch roof.

4.2.7 Rubbing one's hands

The person is confident and in a good mood. It seems like the deal is done.

It is a typical gesture seen by sales people or traders after they signed a deal.

Usually this gesture goes hand in hand with a positive facial expression.

Both hands are rubbing together.

4.2.8 Shaking hands with the hand from above

This is a really arrogant gesture and the person wants to clearly demonstrate that he is stronger and more powerful than the other one.

The other person should gently try to get him off his high horse.

While shaking hands one hand is reached from above so that the other person must directly look at the top of the other person's hand.

4.2.9 Using a hand as bow

The person is trying to make his
way through an imaginary
crowed.

This usually happens when
somebody is walking and he
wants to create some space
around himself or the room in
order to walk through it.

Or when somebody is sitting
down and wants to work around
some outspoken arguments.

One hand is lifted up until right underneath the chin.

The other person can see the edge of the hand.

The hand makes a forward motion.

4.2.10 Playing with a pen

The person is unoccupied or
nervous and cramped.

Maybe he is afraid of something.

If the tip of a pen is pointing at
the other person one could expect some sort of confrontation.

If the person points with the pen toward himself it could mean he is
egotistical.

Absentmindedly playing with a pen in his hand.

The pen turns around and around.

4.2.11 Clenching a fist

The person is holding back his agitation.

He is angry and furious.

A confrontation is expected.

One hand is clenched into a fist.

4.2.12 Waving aside with one's hand

The person wants to discourage others with this gesture: "No, no, no!"

Or: "Don't take me!"

The hand is lifted up and waved back and forth.

The other person can see the palm of his hand. It demonstrates that he does not want to comment the subject at all.

One hand slightly waves aside.

121

4.2.13 Fluttering one's fingers

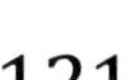

The person wants to understand something but cannot understand or entirely understand the statement made by the speaker.

Verbally it can be translated as follows: "What were you trying to say?"

There is visible impatience with this question.

The other person should try to explain his thoughts with other words one more time.

The fingertips are closed and they are moved towards the head and then up and down from the wrist.

4.2.14 Kissing one's fingertips

The person just kissed his fingertips
and now he is throwing his kiss to another person or into the air.

He is really convinced about a subject
or statement. "Crème de la crème!"
Or: "Great!" Or : "Outstanding!"

The closed fingertips are pulled away from the mouth.

Then the fingertips open outward.

4.2.15 Turning a hand back and forth

In this movement of the hand the fingertips are pointing at the other person who could interpret this as aggression towards him.

The movement of the hand to the right
and left indicates that the statement of
the other person is not accepted at all.

"Well, I don't know."

It also can be an answer to the questions: "How are you doing?" Or:
"Are you making progress with this assignment?"

This answer can be interpreted as follows: "It's all right."

In both cases the other person should put the assignment in different words in order to help to get the work done.

The fingertips of one hand point to the other person.

The hand's position is vertical.

Then the hand moves back and forth to the side.

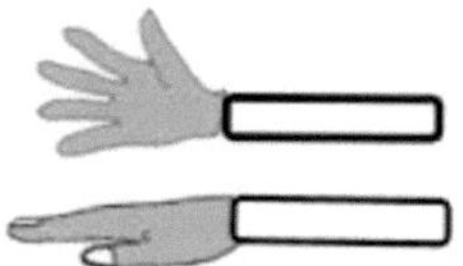

4.2.16 Rotating a hand

This gesture shows skepticism:
"Is that all right, what I just
heard?"

The other person should repeat his statement with different words
and observe the person so he can directly question him if necessary
and determine whether he has a different opinion.

One hand is at the height of the head.

It will then rotate back and forth.

4.2.17 Letting a hand fall

The person is obviously depicting
hitting something and therefore
this movement is seen as a defensive gesture:

"Hmm, just go, what should I do
with it?"

Or: "That's not my thing."

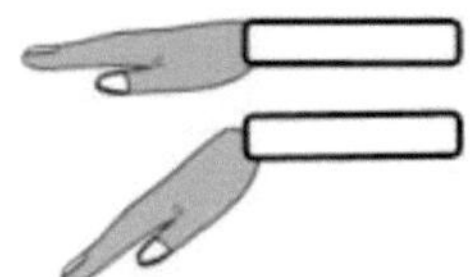

One hand is dropping with a slightly out-stretched arm.

The back of the hand is facing up.

123

4.2.18 Chopping with one hand into the other

This is clearly an aggressive gesture. It means that the argument or statement is "chopped up".

The verbal expression can be: "I just want to make clear ..."

Or: "It's meant this way and no other one!"

The person demonstrates pretty precisely that there is no further discussion about the subject.

If the other person has a contradictory opinion he should avoid that discussion at this moment.

He could say: "Let's talk about it later."

Or: "We will pick up that subject some other time."

One hand is chopping into the palm of hand of the other one.

4.2.19 Beckoning to someone with a hand

The person beckons another person over to him with one hand: "Come closer to me, please."

One hand is a little bit away from the body and the palm of the hand is lifted up.

The hand is waved at someone from the wrist.

4.2.20 Throwing up a hand

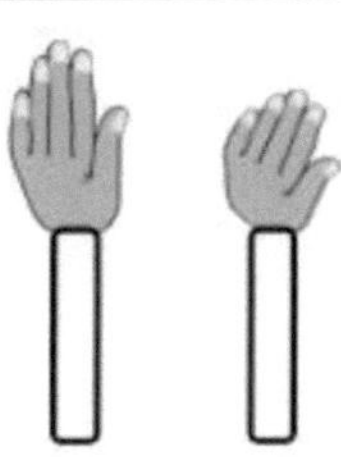

This gesture means that the person throws something over his shoulder. The person does not want or need it anymore and therefore he throws it away.

It is not a positive gesture if a subject or specific case is involved: "I don't care!" Or: "That's not your business!" It demonstrates a certain disinterest.

One hand throws something imaginary over the shoulder.

4.2.21 Holding a hand to one's ear

This gesture can mean that somebody is needed on the telephone or that the respective person would like to use the telephone.

Sometimes the index finger is widely spread to symbolize using an old rotary dial.

In most cases the right hand is lifted up to the ear.

125

4.2.22 Measuring height with a hand

The person demonstrates what the height of something is or another person is.

"The height is approximately so high." This is a neutral and informative gesture

The arm is stretched out and then the hand with its palm to the top moves up and shows a certain height.

4.2.23 Circling one's hand at the head

It means: „He/she is not clear in his head."

One hand is circling in the area of the temple.

4.2.24 Moving a hand up in front of the stomach

The hand is in front of the person's stomach.

The hand moves up and down and if the rhythm of the movements is the same it means: "Hey, back off."

If the rhythm going up is clearly stronger than it means: "Go! Leave me alone!"

The hand is in front of the stomach and moves up and down from the wrist.

4.2.25 Making the hand into a ring

If this gesture is used, then it is a positive statement: "Just fine!"

The person is completely satisfied with the success or subject of the conversation.

Index finger and thumb of one hand create a ring.

The hand is slightly lifted up.

4.2.26 Kissing a ring formed from a hand

The fingertips of the index finger and the thumb form a ring and the person kisses this ring.

It is a positive gesture towards what has happened or what has been said. In colloquial language: "Crème de la crème!"

The index finger and the thumb of one hand create a ring. The person kisses the ring where the fingers come together.

4.2.27 Saluting with a hand

To salute with the hand is actually a military greeting. Sometimes people do that to do a gesture that is meant as a well-intentioned gag.

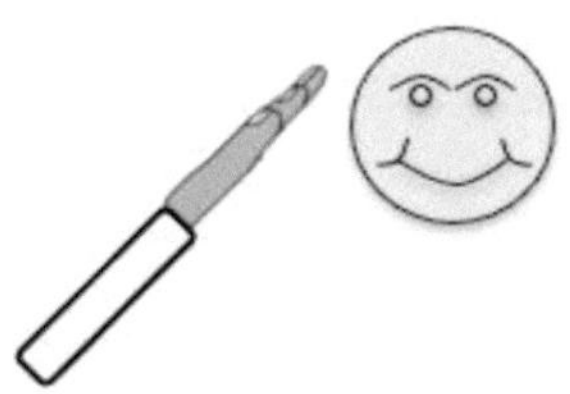

The person greets/salutes obediently towards the other person and he demonstrates compliance or respect towards him.

The closed finger–tips of a flat outstretched hand allusively touch the temple.

4.2.28 Hitting one's own hand

The person punishes himself by hitting on his own hand. "I shouldn't have said/done that!"

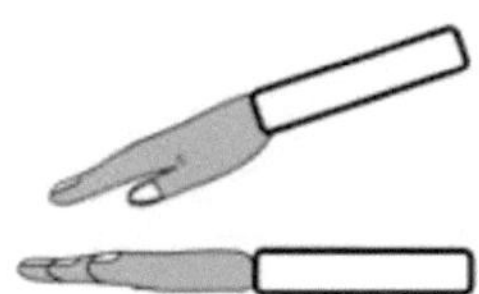

The person realizes that he made a mistake.

The upper hand slightly hits on the stretched out lower hand. The back of the lower hand is facing up.

4.2.29 Writing on one's own hand

For this gesture there are several interpretations possible:

- The person asks for a pencil.

- He wants to sign a document.

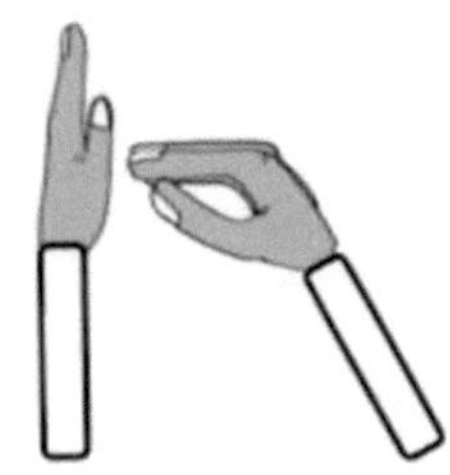

The right hand indicates a writing gesture.

4.2.30 Swinging a hand

This is a more negative gesture intended for the other person.

The person struggles with the conversation: "Hmm, just leave me alone,

I don't want to be associated with that!"

Or: "That's not my thing, I'm not in charge of it."

The slightly out-stretched hand with its back to the top tries to fend something off.

4.2.31 Drinking out of one's hand

The person signals that he is thirsty.

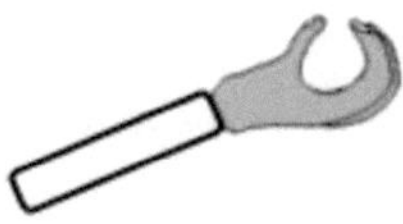

One hand is bringing an imaginary glass to the mouth.

4.2.32 The victory-sign

The person indicates that he
wants to have peace and that
there is no aggressive attitude at
all.

Winston Churchill used this sign very often in public.

It is a neutral or positive gesture for business-partners.

Victory-sign: index and middle finger of the right hand
form a V-sign.

The palm of the hand points into the direction of the other person.

4.2.33 Pushing one's hand forward

Showing the fingertips to another person always signals an
aggressive attitude.

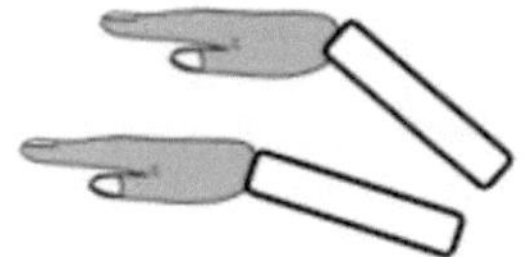

When the person pushes the
hand in the direction of the other
person this gesture is even
stronger.

"I maintain my opinion!"

Or: "I insist on what I already said!"

This gesture is not necessarily meant to be negative for the speaker
because it is possible that he simply tries to convey his opinion.

The flat hand with closed fingers and with the back of the hand facing up, pointing to the other person.

4.2.34 Lifting both hands

Very often this gesture goes hand in hand with a questioning facial expression in order to strengthen it.

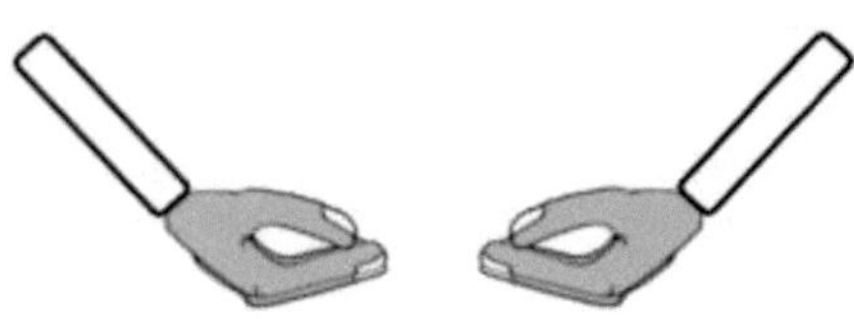

The hands are slightly moving towards the person and he asks: "What do I know?"

The person is not aware of any guilt.

The other person may notice some disinterest.

Both hands are lifted in front of the upper part of the body.

The palms of the hands are facing up and the fingers are slightly bent upward.

4.2.35 Lifting one or both hands

The difference from 4.2.34 is that there is no facial expression that asks a question.

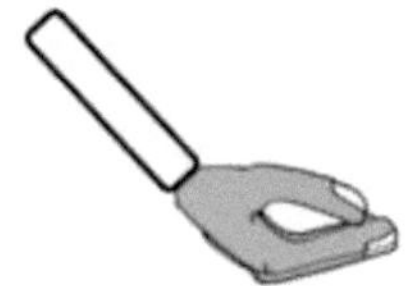

The person demonstrates with this gesture that he is not explicitly telling the truth.

"What do I know?"

One or both hands are lifted up in front of the upper part of the body.

The palms of the hands are facing up and the fingers are slightly bent.

4.2.36 Bundling the fingers together

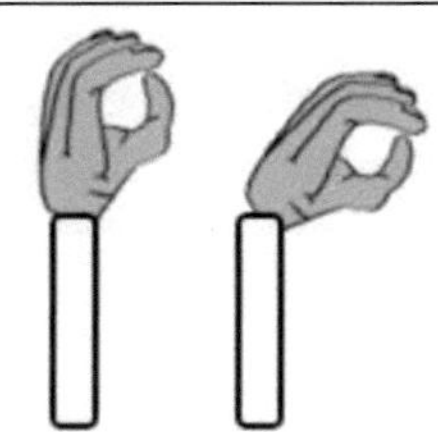

The person illustrates that he is hungry.

All fingertips of one hand are touching each other and then they are moving together from the wrist into the slightly open mouth.

4.2.37 Waving with a hand (1)

The person waves friendly towards another person: "Hello, here I am!"

This is seen as a positive gesture.

The person tries to get somebody else's attention.

The hand is held over the head and it is waving.

4.2.38 Waving with a hand (2)

The person is waving towards another person to say good-bye.

It is a nice and personal gesture which indicates that the two people like each other.

The stretched out hand is waving towards somebody else.

131

4.2.39 Form a choking gesture with one's hands

The person's hands are choking
a fictitious neck.

This is really an aggressive gesture: "I could kill him!"

It is advisable that the other person clears up the situation.

He should try to figure out where the aggression is coming from and
he should try to create a neutral or positive atmosphere again.

Both hands are in a position of a stranglehold in front of the body.

The fingers of both hands are touching each other.

4.2.40 Hands clasping together

The person is asking for help:
"Please, help me; I don't know
what to do!"

The other person should try to
help the person if possible.

The hands are held together as if they are praying.

4.2.41 Opening one's arms crossed in front of the chest

First it is seen as a defensive action and then the body is liberated.

The final movement in this gesture can be expressed as follows: "I am done!"

Or: "It's all over!"

Both forearms are crossed in front of the chest.

Then they are abruptly opened.

4.2.42 Shaking hands

To shake hands creates closeness and intimacy.

Persons who do not like each other usually do not shake hands as well.

Two people shaking hands.

4.2.43 Forming scissors with one's hands

This is a defensive posture. "No, thank you, not for me!" Or: "I don't want anymore!"

The hands are crossing at the wrists and they are held in front of the chest. The palms of the hands show in the direction of the other person. The hands open and close at the wrists several times.

4.2.44 Boxing the palm of the hand

This is a slightly aggressive gesture.

"Well, I will show him what's going on!"

Or: "We'll see!"

Most likely the person will act following these words and gesture and the other person should try to manage the attitude into a direction more comfortable for everybody.

One hand is boxing into the palm of the other hand.

4.2.45 Showing the outstretched palms to someone

One person comes seeking for help from another person. "Please, help me!"

Or: "I am begging you on my knees!"

The other person should try to help him if it is possible.

This gesture is also seen when a speaker for example has lost his train of thought or if he is seeking for consent from the audience.

Both palms of the hands are facing upward and they are stretched out in the direction of the other person.

4.2.46 Kissing the palm of the hand

The person is throwing a hand-kiss in the direction of another person.

"I love you!"

Or: "I like you!"

Or: "Thank you!"

The person kisses the palm of his hand, and then pulls the hand away from the mouth.

4.2.47 Palm of one hand and head looking to the sky

"Dear God, please help me!"

This gesture is some sort of begging gesture where the person is begging for help and support.

It is also used when the other person said something the person does not agree with at all.

This is a way to make fun of the other person.

The palm of the hand is open to the sky.

It is even with the chest.

The head is also looking up toward the sky.

4.2.48 Rubbing the palm of a hand with the heel of the other

This illustrates that somebody is getting pressed or squeezed in between the palm and the heel of hand.

This is an aggressive gesture and can be expressed as follows: "I showed him what was what!"

The heel of the hand is rubbing against the palm of the other hand.

4.2.49 Clapping into each other's palms of the hands

"Done – the contract is signed!"

It is a positive sign. Both business-partners are happy with the con-clusion.

They closed a deal and they seal it with a handshake.

Two persons clapping each other in their palms of the hands.

4.2.50 Hitting the palm of the hand with a fist from underneath

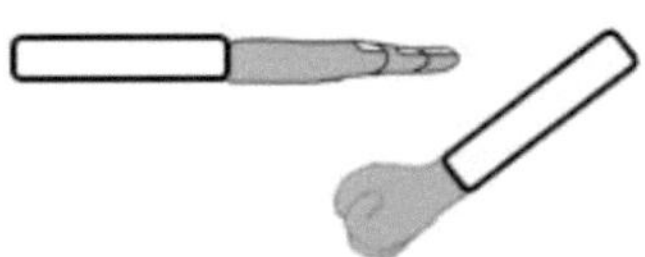

This gesture can display discrimination towards women because it demonstrates violence.

It symbolizes rhythmical moves from a sexual connotation.

The fist of one hand hits from underneath against the palm of the other hand.

4.2.51 Outstretched hand with the palm facing out

This is a demanding and aggressive gesture.

"Give me something!"

137

The palm of the hand is open and is held out in the direction of another person.

4.2.52 Stroking the palm of the hand with the thumb

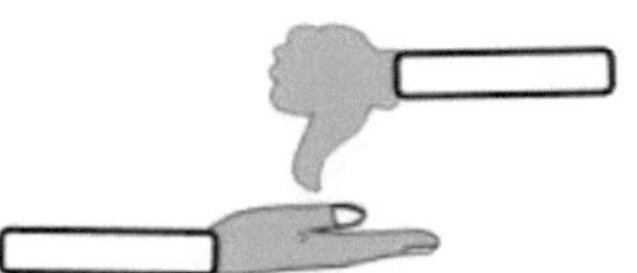

"Looks like you're right!"

Or: "You're going to pay!"

It is meant in a humorous way and demonstrates a malicious joy.

The thumb moves lightly over the palm of the other hand.

4.2.53 Die Lowering out-stretched hands

The person lowers his out-stretched hands which can be expressed verbally as follows: "Not so fast, one thing at a time."

The speaker should evaluate whether he talked too quickly or about the subject or the negotiations and as a result the person could not follow him.

If a seminar leader uses this gesture he wants to keep the group together and get the discussions in order.

Both hands are showing with the palms facing the ground.

The hands are slowly moved a few times in the direction of the ground.

4.2.54 Showing a palm of the hand out and to the front

This gesture demonstrates a defensive behavior. The person holds his hand in front of him so the other person sees the palm of his hand.

He does not want to be offended.
He swears he is telling the truth.

The right hand is stretched out and the palm of the hand facing in the direction of the other person.

4.2.55 Wiping off the palms of the hands

The fingertips point in the direction of the other person and it can be seen as a slightly defensive measure towards him.

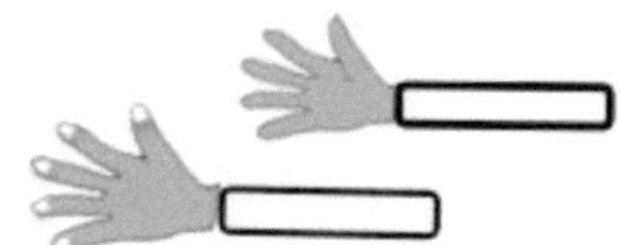

The palms of the hands are wiping on each other which demonstrates: "I wash my hands of it!"

Therefore the person demonstrates that he prefers not to get involved in this situation.

The palms of the hands are rubbed against each other.

The fingertips point in the direction of the other person and the edges of the hand point to the ground.

139

4.2.56 Laying the palms of the hands together

The person is a little bit nervous and is seeking support.

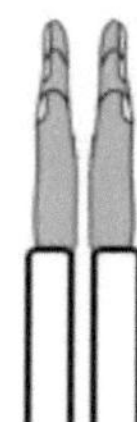

He asks the other person for help and he is almost begging.

If possible the other person should help.

Both palms of the hands are pressed together.

The fingertips point up and forward.

4.2.57 Hiding the thumb

The person tries to reassure himself by sticking his thump inside his fist.

He is close to sealing a deal.

This gesture is also used to wish someone luck (e.g., for sporting events, exams).

"Go for it! All the best!"

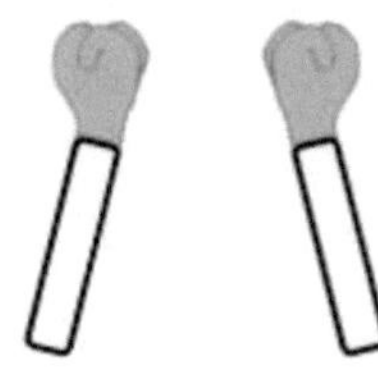

Both thumbs are pressed inside the fists.

4.2.58 Palms of the hands facing forward

The palms of the hand face in the direction of the other person and therefore it is a defensive posture.

Obviously the person expects a confrontation and he tries to defend himself.

"I don't want anything to do with you!"

Or: "Stop, don't get any closer!"

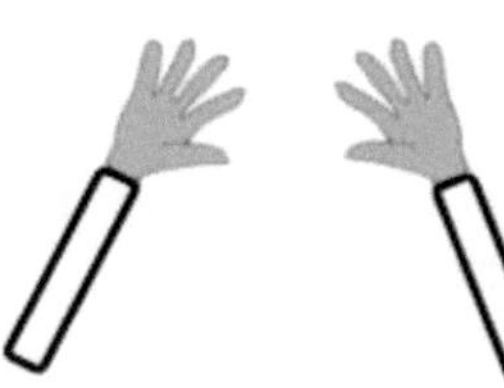

Both arms are held out and the palms of the hands face in the direction of the other person.

4.2.59 Twirling a hand on the side of the body

This hand movement symbolizes theft. Something or an idea has been taken.

The hand is open and it twirls so that it appears as if the fingers are steeling something.

One hand is twirled on the side of the body.

The fingers open and close again during the movement.

4.2.60 Wringing one's hands

This gesture can be seen a little bit aggressive unless it is used as a joke.

It appears that the person wants to wring somebody's neck.

Both hands are formed to a fist.

They are twisted against each other as if they want to wring out a wet towel.

4.2.61 Rubbing the hands in each other

This gesture indicates distress. "I don't know how I should behave and what I should do with my hands."

Or: "I'm sorry about what happened. Unfortunately I can't help."

The hands are slightly cupped together and they are rubbing each other.

141

4.2.62 The palms of the hands facing toward the body

"You're absolutely welcome!"

The arms hug another person.

This is seen as a positive gesture.

Both arms are widely spread away from the body and they hug an imaginary person.

4.2.63 Pushing the palms away

This gesture demonstrates a distance from body to body.

The hands are widely spread. "I have nothing to do with you!"

The person tries to keep a certain distance from the speaker or from the subject.

Both hands are parallel to each other and widely pushed away from the body.

4.2.64 Crossing the wrists

The person he feels as if he has been imprisoned by the other person. "I give myself up."

It is also a sign of repression.

It also can be that the person was caught up in his thoughts and he cannot find his way out.

The wrists are crossed and facing in the direction of the other person.

4.2.65 Touching the heart

There are two possible interpretations:

"God, why did this happen to me?"

Or: "I swear it's the truth!"

In the second interpretation, somebody obviously challenged the statement.

One hand is lying on the left side of the chest.

4.2.66 Sawing at one's throat

The person is obviously under stress and in a bad situation.

With this gesture he wants to express the following: "I have had it up to here!"

He has reached his limit with the unpleasant experiences.

If it continues, he wound "drown".

The hand held flat with the thumb facing the throat, slowly sawing back and forth.

143

4.2.67 Slitting one's throat open

Obviously the person wants to slit the throat of another person.

This gesture is seen as negative and means aggression.

The hand held flat with the thumb facing the throat, fast and jerky moving past the throat.

4.2.68 Clasping one's throat

This is seen as an aggressive gesture as well: "I'd like to choke you!"

It also is possible that the person inflicts this gesture on himself because he just said something wrong and he wants to punish himself.

To clasp the throat with one hand.

4.2.69 Touching the shirt cuff

This is a gesture of embarrassment or dilemma.

The person tries to wipe off imaginary fluff off his cuff.

While doing this, both hands are in front of his body.

As described in other chapters the person tries to protect himself.

"The other people shouldn't realize my precarious position."

It is often seen when a person is on stage in a discussion group or if the person has to walk a long way to the other person.

The index finger and the thumb briefly touch the cuff
of the other arm.

4.2.70 Clenching a fist

The person wants to demonstrate his power and strength with this gesture as well as to the other people that he is not afraid of confrontation with them.

Clenching a fist, may include showing and shaking it.

4.2.71 Twirling one's fist in front of the mouth

A person who twirls his fist in front of his mouth wants to say that he knows something that it is not allowed.

Therefore the threat with the fist is meant toward himself.

The fist is twirled once in front of his mouth.

4.2.72 Hitting a fist in the air

This gesture demonstrates strength because nobody really is beaten.

The gesture is often used by sportsmen when they win or when they want to motivate themselves

One fist hits into the air.

145

4.2.73 Threatening with a fist

To threaten with one fist is clearly a sign of
aggression.

The threatening fist is shown to the other person.

4.2.74 Shaking both fists above the head

This is a demonstration of feeling
like a winner: "We are the best,
we won!"

Or: "We are the champions!"

Both fists are shaking above the head with outstretched arms.

4.3 Finger, thumb, ankle

4.3.1 Holding up the index finger (as if in school)

Somebody holds up the finger in the air and wants to educate or to lecture the other person.

The index finger of one hand is lifted vertically in the air.

4.3.2 Snapping one's fingers

There are several possible explanations:

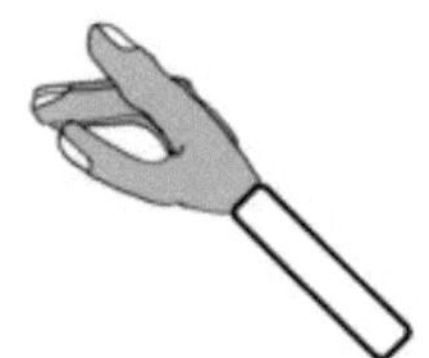

- Snap with the fingers once: "Ah, I got an idea."

- Snap with the fingers twice: "Well, where's the idea?"

- Snap with the fingers several times: "I'd like to speak."

147

Thumb, index and middle finger make a snapping noise.

4.3.3 Knocking on the desk with an index finger

The person tries to get attention by knocking his index finger on the desk top and the current conversation is likely interrupted.

The person tries to emphasize his statement.

He insists on his opinion. Obviously he feels confident with what he just said.

The index finger knocks on the desk top a few times.

4.3.4 Drumming fingers

The person is impatient and nervous.

He wants to say something and/or interrupt the discussion.

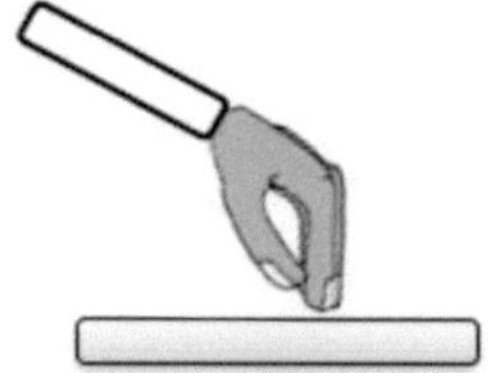

The other person should let him speak as soon as possible or tell him that it will be his time to speak up soon.

If the drumming happens absentmindedly the person is thinking about something else.

Four fingers are drumming on the desk top.

4.3.5 Knocking with the knuckles on wood

Widespread superstition means that someone needs to knock on wood to prevent from something unpleasant happening to him.

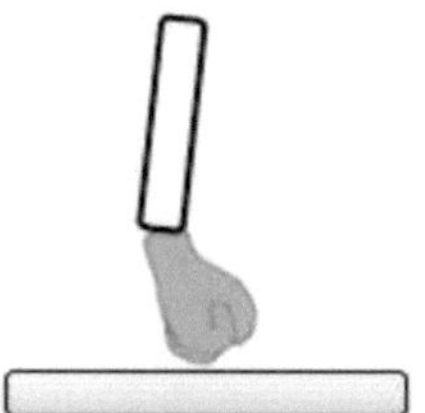

"It hasn't happen to me but ..."

Four knuckles of one hand are knocking on wood.

4.3.6 Pressing the finger-tips together

The person is trying to make a point.

He wants to specify and summa-rize his statement.

"What I want to say is ..."

All fingertips of one hand are pressed together.

4.3.7 Raising up the middle finger

This is a gesture that demonstrates that the person has a very bad opinion of the other person.

This gesture has rude sexual undertones.

It absolutely needs to be avoided in a serious conversation.

The middle finger is raised up ("to flip off somebody" or "give the finger").

4.3.8 Forming a circle with one's index finger and thumb

149

There are several possible explanations:

- Okay, everything's fine."

- To give somebody a clear-cut statement: "It is like I said …"

- Negative meaning: "You're nothing (a "zero")!"

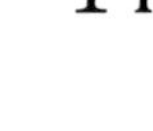

Index finger and thumb touch on the fingertips and form a circle.

4.3.9 Drawing circles with the index finger

If the circling is pointing down,
the person wants to sign something (e.g., a contract, a bill in a
restaurant).

If the circling finger points towards the front, to the side, or up, it
means later, tomorrow, or in the future.

"Let's talk about it on Monday again."

The index finger symbolizes a circling movement.

While doing that it points towards the desk top or up in the air.

4.3.10 Holding one's hand up

One person holds his hand up in
order to get attention (e.g., during a discussion or in class) because he want to participate or
say something.

The index finger of one hand points up.

The heel of the hand points into the direction of the speaker.

4.3.11 Pointing with an out-stretched finger at another person

This is a very impolite and ac-cusing gesture.

The person is explicitly pointing at somebody else in order to ac-cuse him of something or to compromise him; (similar to 4.3.13: *Pointing the index finger at somebody)* but this gesture is much stronger.

The index finger of the stretched out arm points at another person.

4.3.12 Pointing with an out-stretched finger at some-thing

The person points clearly at something.

"I mean THAT."

Usually the object is far enough from the showing person so it can-not be mixed up with gesture of 4.3.11.

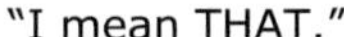

The index finger of the stretched out arms points at something.

4.3.13 Pointing the index finger at somebody

The person's index finger points offensively at another person.

It can be seen as an accusation. "He did it!"

Or: "What YOU said is ..."

The speaker should avoid this kind of gesture because it appears like he is lecturing.

To point with one's index finger directly at another person.

4.3.14 Threaten with the index finger

The person is making a threat. "Let me tell you something ..."

It also can be used in a judging manner: "I absolutely disagree with what you did!"

The index finger of one hand points up vertically.

The other person can look at the back side of the hand.

The index finger is moving back and forward.

4.3.15 Stretching out the index finger far

The person wants to demonstrate that he is "Number One".

This behavior can be seen as a winning gesture.

The index finger points in the air. The arm is stretched out far.

The hand is also waving at the wrist.

4.3.16 Beckoning someone with an index finger

The person beckons somebody else towards him.

"Just come closer ..."

One index finger beckons another person to come closer.

The other person sees the angled hand from the front.

4.3.17 Rubbing the index fingers against each other

The person demonstrates malicious joy. "Ha, ha! - good that it happened to you!"

This gesture is mostly used to be funny or as a joke.

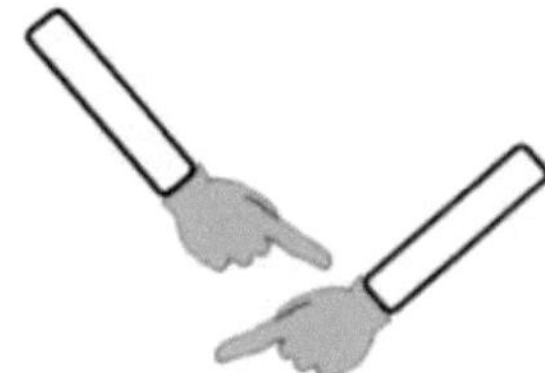

One index finger is lying on the index finger of the other hand and it rubs down from the back of the hand to the fingertips several times.

153

4.3.18 Moving an index finger back and forth

This gesture demonstrates nega-
tion.

"No, no, that's not correct!"

Or: "You shouldn't do that!"

The index finger is moved back and forth.

The other person is looking at the heel of the hand.

4.3.19 Moving the index fingers together

The person demonstrates there is a problem. "The problem is that …"

At the end of the movement, the fingertips of the index fingers touch
each other and that symbolizes that there is no further movement
because there is resistance, a problem, or a barrier.

Both index fingers are moving towards each other until their
fingertips touch each other.

The fingers will stay in that position for a moment.

4.3.20 Sucking on one's index finger

The person tries to make himself smaller and younger than he actually is.

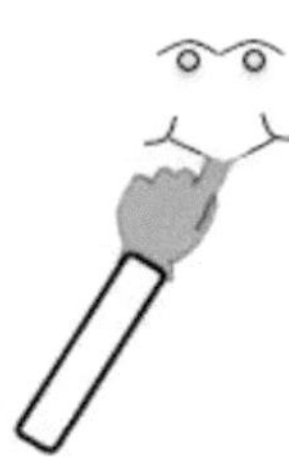

He puts his index finger inside his mouth like a child.

He knows that children are weak and therefore are untouchable in comparison to an adult.

This gesture means: "I don't know. Please leave me alone."

One index finger is inside the mouth and is sucked on.

4.3.21 Put the finger on the mouth

There are two different possible explanations when somebody puts his index finger on the mouth.

- If the person closes his eyes and drops the head, then it is likely he is shy and/or unconfident.
- If the person looks up, he is thinking about something or he is trying to remember something.

One index finger lies on the closed lower lip.

4.3.22 Cigarette fingers

The person illustrates how a smoker moves his cigarette towards his mouth.

Obviously the person wants to smoke a cigarette.

The index and middle finger form a "V" and move towards the mouth.

4.3.23 Hiding one's thumb

This is a sexual gesture. It is not advisable to use it in a serious conversation.

Sometimes the wrist moves back and forward while using this gesture.

The bent thumb is tucked in between the index and middle finger of a fist.

4.3.24 Target with the index and middle fingers

The person targets with his fingers toward another person like he is holding a pistol.

Index and middle finger form the gun barrel.

This gesture means: "I'll shoot you."

Fortunately, this gesture is only used to be funny or as a joke.

Index and middle finger are lying next to each other.

They are stretched out and they are pointing at another person.

4.3.25 Twiddling thumbs

This gesture demonstrates the well-known "twiddle one's thumbs."

The person is bored and shows that he has nothing better to do at the moment.

Obviously the other person should give him an assignment.

Both hands are clasped together and the thumbs are twiddling around each other.

4.3.26 Thumb's up

This is really positive sign for a good result: "That was great!"

Or: "Outstanding – A+."

A good gesture for a conversation.

The thumb of one hand points up.

The other fingers are curled onto the palm of the hand.

4.3.27 Thumb's down

This gesture demonstrates a negative result: "What you did was really not that good."

The thumb of one hand points down.

The other fingers are curled onto the palm of the hand.

4.3.28 Sucking on one's thumb

The person is nervous and tries to make himself smaller than he really is.

He is sucking on his thumb like a baby.

Most likely the person just has not told the entire truth and is thinking about how to get out of this precarious situation.

Sucking on the thumb of one hand.

4.3.29 Pointing with the thumb toward another person

This is an insulting gesture.

"Look at that person over there …"

The person wants to express through this gesture his deprecation towards the other person.

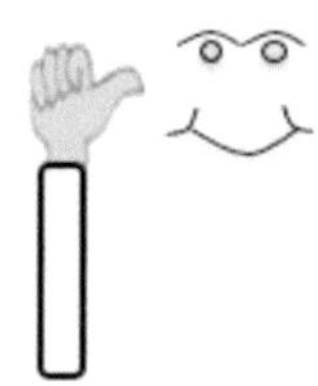

The thumb points usually above his shoulder towards another person.

4.3.30 Biting one's finger nails

The person is thoughtful and does not say anything.

He is trying to calm down his fear by chewing on his finger nails.

The fingertips of one hand are lying on the lower lip.

The person is chewing on his finger nails.

4.3.31 Forming a claw with one's fingers

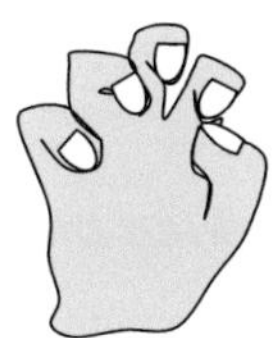

This is more a gesture used for fun or as a joke and it means: "I'm a predator and I'd like to grab you …"

The person obviously does not consent with what the other person just said or did.

Showing the other person the form of a claw by moving the fingers and the thumb together.

159

4.3.32 Fanning with the fingers

The person makes clear that he just burned his fingers.

They are supposed to cool off by fanning them through fresh air.

Also means that something embarrassing has happened or he has done something where difficulties are expected

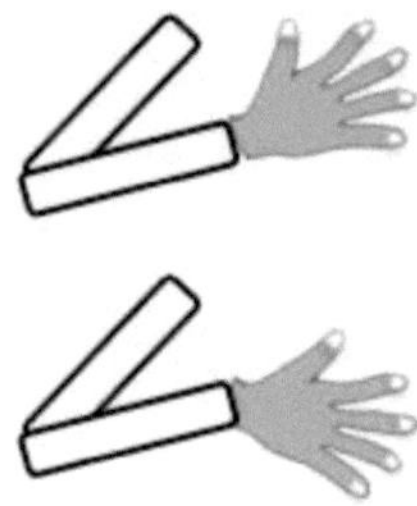

The fingers are spread to the wide and they are fanning through the air.

4.3.33 Shaking the fingers

The person did something he wishes he could take back.

He would like to "throw away" his fingers that were used make that mistake.

"How could I do that?" could be the question going together with the gesture.

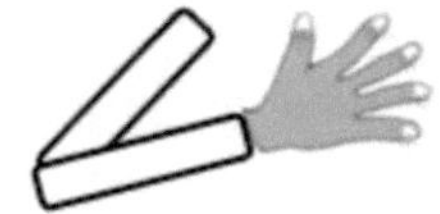

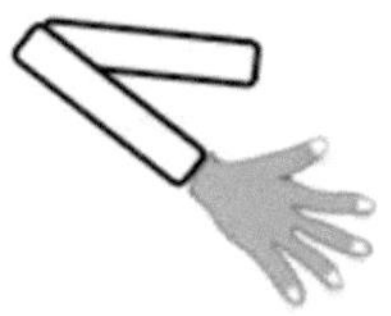

The fingers of one hand are shaking the hand away from the body.

4.3.34 Chattering fingers

This finger gesture symbolizes a chattering quick tongue.

"Much ado about nothing."

The gesture is very often seen behind the back of the person it is referring to.

When it is pointed into the direction of the meant person is usually goes together with the verbal expression: "Hogwash!"

All fingers are parallel to each other.

They are moving up and down towards the thumb several times.

4.3.35 Crossing two fingers

This gesture is usually hid behind somebody's back when the person does not tell the truth.

Symbolically the two fingers form a cross to "undo" the lie.

Index and middle finger of one hand are lying across each other forming a cross.

4.3.36 Rubbing the thumb on the fingertips

This gesture means that something cost money or that there is money.

The thumb rubs on top of the fingertips of the index and middle finger of the same hand several times back and forth.

161

4.3.37 Waving with one's fingers

This finger gesture demonstrates a wave. It is a friendly good-bye to somebody else.

It also can be a funny statement "And good-bye!"

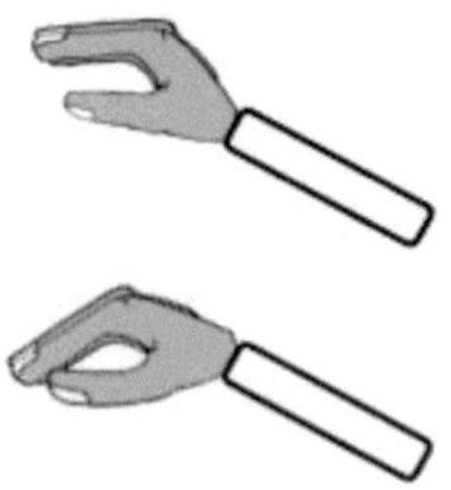

One hand is held up.

The palms of the hands are pointing in the direction of the other person and the fingers are clapping open and closed.

4.3.38 Polishing one's finger nails

The person wants to symbolize that he is grooming himself.

This gesture also demonstrates that the person can afford to manicure his nails while other people are working or thinking about something important.

Therefore, it expresses that the person believes that he is smarter than the other people because he already knows the conclusion.

This gesture is mostly used as a joke and extremely exaggerated.

One hand with bent fingers is held in front of the open mouth.

Then the finger nails are breathed on and polished with the clothes.

Chapter 5

163

Unlocking the secrets of body language: The legs

5.1 Legs

5.1.1 Crossing one's legs towards the other person

This posture is positive.

164

The person is sitting down relaxed and he demonstrates empathy in the direction where the foot of the crossed leg points to.

This is a good sign for the other person.

The person is open to gather new information and has a positive attitude towards the subject.

There is empathy toward the other person.

One leg is lying casually on top of the other one.

The tip of the foot points in the direction of the other person.

5.1.2 Crossing one's legs away from the other person

This posture is also positive.

The person is sitting down re-laxed and expressed a general kind of empathy.

It reflects a good sign for the other person because the person has a positive attitude towards the open atmosphere and towards the sub-ject.

One leg is lying casually on top of the other one.

The tip of the foot does not point in the direction of the other person.

5.1.3 Crossing cramped legs

The person is holding one leg tight with the other one.

Usually the person is insecure, uncertain, or unsteady.

In very rare cases this is seen as a relaxed posture for ladies.

In first case, the other person should try to establish a fearless atmos-phere so the person can relax.

A leg is curled around the other leg.

The toes are tucked around the calf of the other leg.

5.1.4 Spreading and stretching out legs while sitting down

This gesture demonstrates non-acceptance as a response to something that happened earlier.

Depending on how far the upper part of the body is leaned back, the person is trying to keep a certain distance to event or the other person.

The legs are parallel and widely stretched out while sitting down.

The upper part of the body is leaned back.

5.1.5 Laying a foot on the other leg while the knee points towards the other person

This posture is generally rejection.

If the knee points in the direction of the other person it is a direct rejection of the other person or his statement.

One leg stands on the ground.

The other foot lies on top of the knee.

The knee points in the direction of the other person.

5.1.6 Laying a foot on the other leg while the foot point towards the other person

This posture is also seen as negative and as rejection.

In some cultures it is even seen as extremely insulting if the sole of the foot faces other people.

It can create an unpleasant atmosphere which hampers the start of a conversation.

One leg stands on the ground.

The other one lies on top of the knee.

The sole of the foot faces in the direction of the other person.

5.1.7 One's legs are widely spread apart

This is a posture which is generally seen negatively.

Especially for men, it demonstrates their macho posture which is sometimes desired.

The body leaning back is an expression of being guarded.

The other person should try to see this person as a human being. As soon as he closes the legs, he is able to gather information.

The legs are widely spread apart.

The feet are standing on the ground and the upper part of the body is leaned back.

5.1.8 Stroking one's leg

The person is stroking his own leg.

Most likely his sub-consciousness is telling him: "I'd like if the other person touches me."

For the other person this is a positive posture because the person obviously has empathy towards the other person or the subject.

Absent-mindedly rubbing or stroking over one leg.

5.1.9 Clasping one's leg

This is a rejecting posture.

The person is trying to hold on to himself and does not let any information get close to him.

It is difficult to convince him in this particular situation.

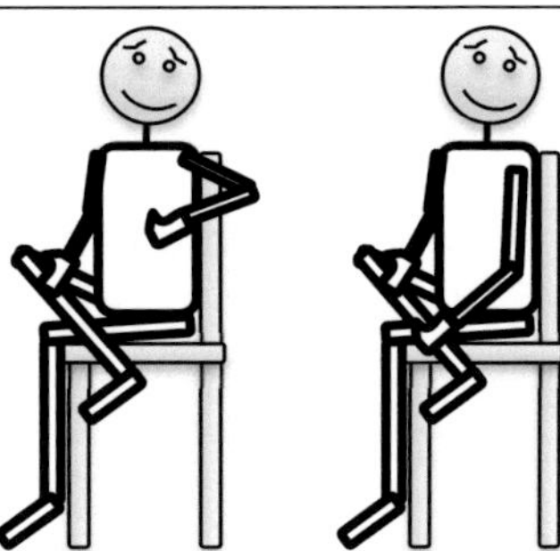

The other person should try to choose a neutral subject and, later on, when the posture changed, get back to the point they are talking about right now.

One leg is standing on the ground.

The other one is lying on the first leg.

One or both hands are holding the upper leg at the shin.

5.1.10 Crossing one's legs

The person is relaxed and does not see any kind of threats or confrontation coming.

To jump up or run away is difficult from this posture.

It is a positive sign for the other person.

The legs are slightly stretched away from the body and they are crossing at the calves.

5.1.11 Closed legs

The person is listening attentively and relaxed as long as the legs are not pressed next to each other.

If the legs would be pressed together, it would demonstrate that he is uptight.

The first posture is positive for the other person because the person gathers the information attentively and he processes it.

While sitting, both legs are parallel to each other and the feet are on the ground.

169

5.1.12 Slapping the thighs

This body movement is often ac-
companies a loud agreeing out-
cry.

The person slaps his thighs because he is surprised or inspired
by an idea, a joke, or information.

If it would be negative this would be the end of the conversation:
"So, that's enough! I'm done!"

The person would directly get up and leave.

While sitting down, one or both hands slap thighs.

5.2 Feet

5.2.1 Teetering on the feet while standing up

The person demonstrates that he is bored or that he is thinking about something other than the subject.

Most likely he would like to do something else or leave.

It is a negative sign for the other person and he should try as soon as possible to start another interesting activity or subject for the person.

While standing, teetering on both feet.

5.2.2 Teetering the feet while sitting down

The teetering with feet while sitting downs is also a bad sign for the other person, just like while standing up.

While sitting down, teetering with both feet.

5.2.3 Crossing legs while sitting down

The person is attentive and re-laxed and he has no expectation of confrontation.

There is a small tendency to-wards holding himself in order to hide a slight uncertainness.

It is difficult to jump up and run away out of this posture.

The legs are crossed at right-angles and folded underneath the chair.

5.2.4 Twisting feet around the leg of a chair

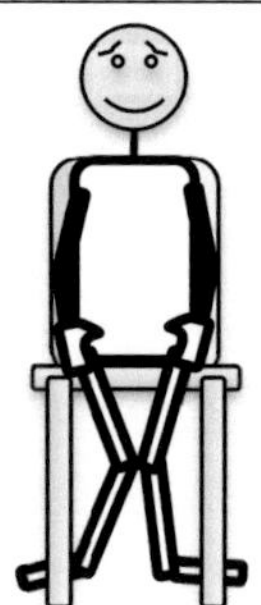

The person demonstrates a pos-ture of enormous insecurity.

He is trying to hold himself onto the legs of the chair and he wishes he was not here.

Unfortunately he has to persevere where he is right now.

Both legs are underneath the chair.

Each foot clamps from behind one of the legs of the chair.

5.2.5 Stepping one foot back while sitting down

The person is relatively alert and he is waiting for an opportunity to get up or to speak and guide the conversation.

It is not possible to jump up and run away with this posture.

The other person could actively listen to the person in order to figure out what the person really wants.

Both legs are bent.

One leg is stepped back underneath the chair and is bracing on the tip of the foot.

The other leg is in front of the chair.

5.2.6 Die Fußspitzen zeigen beim Walking "pigeon-toed"

This body movement is seen as slightly uncertain or as a little bit of a person who is self-conscious.

It is a posture that is coming out of one's sub-consciousness and does not have influence on a conversation.

While walking, the tips of the feet point a little bit to the inside.

5.2.7 Walking with the tips of the toes pointed outward

If the tips of the feet point to the outside most likely the person has an open and self-assured attitude towards life.

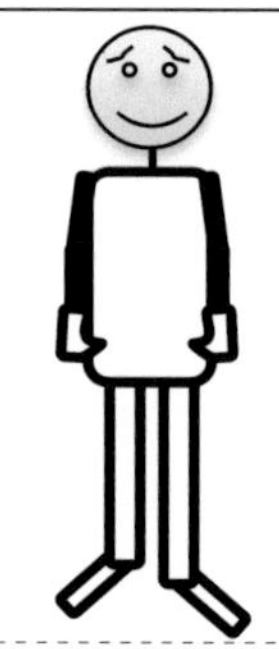

While walking the tips of the feet point a little bit to the outside.

5.2.8 Tapping a foot

Tapping with one's foot symbolizes impatience; maybe dissatisfaction with what has been said.

Most likely the person wants to do or say something.

The other person should give him the opportunity to respond.

Otherwise he will find his way to actively interrupt the conversation and that could be distracting.

While sitting, one foot is tapping while the heel stays on the ground.

174

5.2.9 Tucking a foot behind a leg (1)

The person tries to hold himself back with one foot hanging on to his own body.

He is not confident, is nervous and feels uncomfortable.

The other person should try to create a positive atmosphere as soon as possible.

While sitting down, one foot is tucked behind the calf of the other leg.

5.2.10 Im Tucking a foot be-hind a leg (2)

With this posture, it is hard to maintain balance while standing up. The posture demonstrates the same as in 5.2.9.

Sometimes somebody tries to disguise this posture through scratching on the leg.

It is usually seen when one person can lean with his hand on some-thing (e.g., a lectern).

While standing up, one foot is tucked behind the calf of the other leg.

5.2.11 Teetering with one's feet

The person is bashful and feels caught.

This is very often the case if another person finds out the background of a question.

The teetering of the feet is a sign that somebody would like to run away.

Just in general, teetering feet is not a negative body movement because the person has basically a positive attitude towards the subject or the other person.

While sitting down, teetering with one or both feet up and down.

The heels stay on the ground or one heel is lying on the other leg.

Chapter 6

177

Foreign language of your body

Mistakable gestures

*"Man has much power of discourse which for the most part is vain and false;
animals have but little, but it is useful and true,
and a small truth is better than a great lie."*
Leonardo da Vinci, Italian visionary
(1452 - 1519)

Does your body speak a foreign language? – Different interpretation of your body language abroad

With the help of body language, we can to express and demonstrate what we feel and what we want.

It is possible to impact dialogues just through gestures. Famous pantomimes show it to us all the time.

Over the centuries man has changed to emphasize gestures with corresponding words.

But – it is well known that Germans speak a different language than Chinese. Or Brazilians or the Congolese and so on and so on.

Therefore, we should not been surprised that some body language and gestures are "translated" completely differently in certain countries.

A short selection of some gestures demonstrate that they are interpreted differently abroad than in Germany.

Therefore, be careful using gestures abroad so that there are no misunderstandings and possible disputes with others who have a different cultural background.

Thumbs up

For Germany, it is a positive sign that demonstrates a successful result: "You did a good job."

Or: "Great!" A really good gesture for a conversation.

In China, this gesture shows the number 5; in Indonesia, it stands for the number 6.

In Russia, this gesture is offensive and in Iran, this is a very bad insult.

In Australia and Nigeria it just means "get lost!"

In Turkey and in Greece it is an obscene gesture to solicit sex.

At the same time, moving the thumb moves up and down means homosexual sex.

179

Everything OK?

In the United States and in Germany, it means "terrific, okay".

In Italy, Spain, Greece and Russia it means anal orifice; therefore a very bad insult.

In France, Belgium and, Tunisia, people harass others as being a 'zero', 'nothing' or something worthless.

In Japan, this gesture symbolizes 'money'.

Fist

In most cultures, to threaten
someone with a fist is a clearly
aggressive sign.

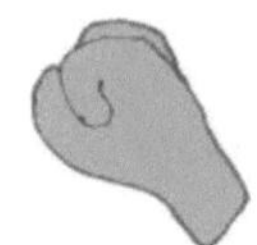

The person is holds back his aggression but he is angry and
ready to 'beat somebody up'.

In Arabian cultures, however, it can be understood as an invitation for
sex.

Victory

This person shows that he wants
peace and that he is not in a
mood to attack someone.

Sir Winston Leonard Spencer-Churchill (brit. prime minister, 1874 –
1965) often used this sign publicly.

It is a neutral to positive gesture to others.

In Greece, it is seen as a very bad insult.

If you turn around your hand it is an equivalent to "flipping someone
off" or "give someone the finger".

This applies not only to Great Britain but also to Australia and Malta.

Showing your shoe sole

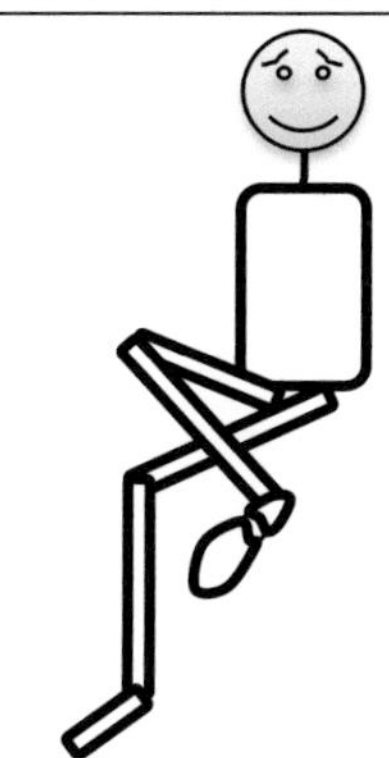

This posture is viewed as negative or denying and also as blocking someone.

In countries with a majority of Muslim faith it is a very bad insult to show someone the sole of your shoes.

It is even possible that others would furiously leave the room if he/she realizes the gesture was meant for him/her.

To stick one's tongue out

In Germany, this is meant as an insult and disrespectful to the person who is being shown the tongue.

This gesture is very negative.

In a relaxed and familiar environment, it also can be used as 'funny' gesture.

However, in Tibet, you can interpret this gesture as a friendly welcome.

To have bats in the belfry

In Germany, your intelligence is questionable.

However, in the United States this gesture means that someone is especially intelligent.

„I am up to my neck in it" (Someone is up to one's neck in it)

The hand is held calmly.

At the moment, the person is in a stressful and/or bad situation or condition.

With this hand gesture he wants to demonstrate that he is has "had it up to here".

It demonstrates that the highest degree of an uncomfortable situation or condition is reached.

If it keeps on going this direction the person is 'drowning'.

Or worse, if the hand moves laterally, it means that the person wants to cut someone's throat.

Therefore, the throat-cutting gesture can be seen as very aggressive.

In Poland, this gesture means that someone had a lot of alcohol to drink and therefore, the person is drunk.

Knocking with one fist on the other palm

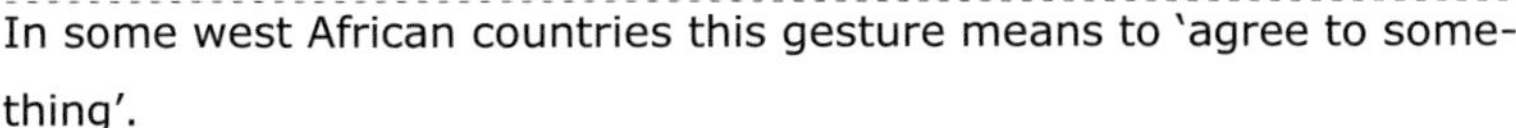

In Germany, it means "Let's go!"

Or: "We will really show them what we can do!"

In some west African countries this gesture means to 'agree to something'.

In Chile and some Arabic countries, it is an invitation for consensual sex.

„Don't point with your pointer finger at someone!"

It is not very nice or polite gesture and it accuses someone.

It is pointed explicitly at another person in order to charge, compromise or embarrasses someone.

In Thailand or Nepal it is seen as a very bad insult and in South Africa as a gesture to start a fight.

183

The hand as a pistol

The fingertip of your pointer finger is targeting another person.

It is some sort of an accusation. "That one did it!"

Or: „Whatever you have said …"

In China, this gesture shows the number 8.

If you are not sure about the nonverbal communication of someone else, it is best to ask this person directly.

It is best to clear up the uncertainty this way instead of offending someone.

Index

185

Annex

Editor and translator

Thomas Schommers holds an A.L.M. in Sustainability and Environmental Management from Harvard University and a B.A. (honours) in Asian Pacific Business Administration from the University of Hertfordshire, UK.

He also is a certified Business Mediator by the Chamber of Commerce and Industry in Munich and a certified China-Manager by the Chamber of Commerce and Industry in Hannover, Germany.

Currently, he works for ISR – International School on the Rhine gGmbH, Germany in the field of public affairs, public relations and marketing.

He is a member of the Curriculum Advisory Board of the Maastricht School of Management, NL.

Since 2007, he has been the team-building coach of their Executive MBA program (in cooperation with Cologne Business School, Germany) and MBA program.

He is an associate lecturer at University of Applied Sciences Bremen for "Doing Business in China." He is the President of the German-American Association Neuss.

He was the head of "Studium Generale" at European University of Applied Sciences (EUFH). At EUFH, he was also an associate lecturer for management/negotiation techniques with Asian people, focusing on the Chinese 36 Stratagems and Sun Tzu, project and change management.

In 2005, he began working for Horst-Hanisch-Seminare Bonn, Germany as freelance coach on Asian issues and on coaching, etiquette, team building, and corporate identity.

He has translated from German to English and edited the book "Discussion – Mastering the Skills of Moderation" by Horst Hanisch.

Additionally, he has worked as a freelance consultant, researcher, and management coach. He has completed projects for the European University of Applied Sciences, Germany, Cologne Business School, Germany; Henley Management College, UK; Maastricht School of Management, Netherlands; Sophia University, Tokyo, Japan; bci - best connection international, Germany, Business Management Services (U.S. agent of KKU), U.S.A.; The Lausanne Consulting Group, UK; United Parcel Service, Germany, the U.S. Consulate General in Düsseldorf, Germany and the U.S. Embassy in Berlin, Germany.

190

12 Ratgeber in der kleinen Knigge-Reihe

Der kleine … -Knigge [2100]

Anstands- und Banausen-…
Business- und Kunden-…
Büro- und Kollegen-…
Gäste- und Gastgeber-…
Gesellschafts- und Freunde-…
Outfit- und Stil-…
Interkulturelle- und Auslands-…
Bewerbungs- und Vorstellungs-…
Event- und Feste-…
Gastro- und Tischsitten-…
Speisen- und Exoten-…
Trinkkultur- und Getränke-…

Je 88 Seiten

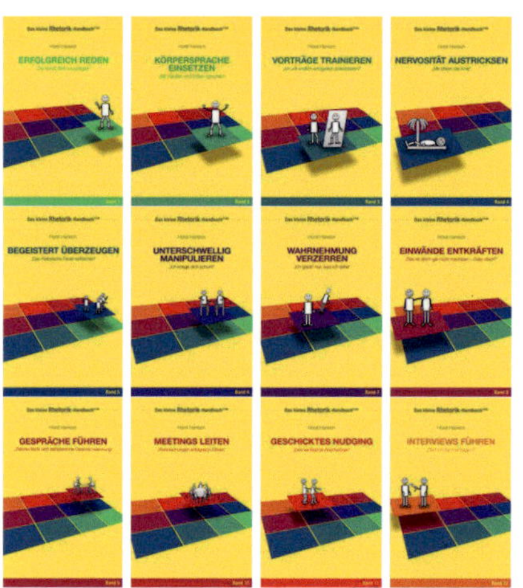

Das kleine Handbuch der Rhetorik [2100]

Erfolgreich reden „Die Kunst, flott vorzutragen"
Körpersprache einsetzen „Mit Händen und Füßen sprechen"
Gezielt trainieren „Ich will endlich erfolgreich präsentieren!"
Nervosität austricksen „Mir zittern die Knie"
Begeistert überzeugen „Das rhetorische Feuer entfachen"
Unterschwellig manipulieren „Ich kriege dich schon!"
Wahrnehmung verzerren „Ich glaub' nur, was ich sehe."
Einwände entkräften „Das ist doch gar nicht machbar! – Oder doch?"
Gespräche führen „Zielorientierte und zeitsparende Gesprächslenkung"
Meetings leiten „Besprechungen erfolgreich führen"
Geschicktes Nudging „Das versteckte Anschubsen"
Interviews führen „Darf ich Sie mal fragen?"
Je 100 Seiten

Das Märchen der …

professionellen Argumentation
harmlosen Fragen
sauberen Wahrheit
vertrauenswürdigen Fairness

… in der Rhetorik [2100]
Je 100 Seiten

4 Ratgeber in der Ego-Management-Reihe

Persönlichkeits-Management – Ego-Knigge 2100 Soft Skills, Selbst-Reflexion und Selbst-Bewusstsein

Stress-Management – Ego-Knigge 2100 Lampenfieber, Stressoren, Gerüchte, Mobbing, Burnout, Stressvermeidung

Zeit-Management – Ego-Knigge 2100 Umgang mit der Zeit, Organisation von Arbeitsabläufen, Perfektionismus, Zielsetzung

Gedächtnis-Management – Ego-Knigge 2100 Gehirn, Intelligenz, Schwachsinn – Hochbegabung, Gedächtnis, Lerntechniken.

Jeder Ratgeber 104 Seiten, A5, kartoniert

4 Ratgeber der Reihe Lebenseinstellung

Aberglauben-Knigge 2100 Von schwarzen Katzen, der linken Hand des Teufels und den Glücksbringern
Lügen- und Egoismus-Knigge 2100 Überleben durch Flunkern, Schummeln und Täuschen! Macht, Respekt, Wertschätzung? Lebenslüge und Lebensschutz
Glücks-Knigge 2100 Vom Glücklichsein, positiven Denken und von Freundschaften
Angst- und Optimismus-Knigge 2100 Die Furcht beherrschen, Ängste nutzen und positiv durchs Leben gehen.

Jeder Ratgeber 216 Seiten, A5, kartoniert

3 Ratgeber Bräutigam, Braut und Brautpaar

Bräutigam-Knigge 2100 Verlobung und Polterabend, Schwiegereltern und das Ja-Wort, Hochzeits-Outfit und Hochzeits-Kutsche

Braut-Knigge 2100 Brautkleid und Accessoires, Das große Hochzeitsfest, Höhepunkte und Hochzeitstanz

Brautpaar-Knigge 2100 Historisches und Sonderbares, Planung und Organisation, Aberglaube und Hochzeitsbräuche.

Jeder Ratgeber 104 Seiten, A5, kartoniert

3 Ratgeber Selbst-Coaching

Selbstbewusstsein Knigge 2100 Ich bin, ich kann, ich will. Das eigene Leben bestimmen, Soft Skills, The Winner 1.

Selbstwertgefühl Knigge 2100 Steh auf! Werde aktiv! Zeige Profil! Das eigene Leben beeinflussen, Motivation, The Winner 2.

Selbstoptimierung Knigge 2100 Optimistischer, attraktiver, authentischer. Das eigene Leben gestalten, Ansprüche, The Winner 3.

Jeder Ratgeber 120 Seiten, A5, kartoniert

Leben und Lifestyle

Adam allein auf der Welt Knigge 2100 Ein Buch mit Bildern vom ersten Menschen, seinen Gedanken und seiner Körpersprache, 104 Seiten, A5, ca. 155 Fotos

Jugend-Knigge 2100 Knigge für junge Leute und Berufseinsteiger, 152 Seiten

Alters-Knigge 2100 Abgehängt und abgeschoben? Altersdiskriminierung? Akzeptanz des Älterwerdens!, 152 Seiten

Zukunfts-Knigge 2100 Verfall der Sitten und Verlust der Wertschätzung? Umgangsformen in 100 Jahren. Zusammenleben mit Menschen, Maschinen und menschenähnlichen Robotern, 172 Seiten A5 kartoniert

KI-Knigge 2100 Leben mit der Künstlichen Intelligenz! Veränderungen im realen Umgang?, 196 Seiten A5 kartoniert

Wertschätzung-Knigge 2100 Gleichberechtigung, Gender und Respekt, Sexuelle Orientierung, Umgang bei Diskriminierung und Mobbing, 152 Seiten A5

Hochzeits-Knigge 2100 Hochzeitsbräuche, Geschenke, Brautjungfer, Trauung, Festgäste und Festmahl, 310 Seiten A5

Ü65- und Senioren-Knigge 2100 Die junge Alten und die alten Jungen, Kommunikation und Verständnis zwischen den Generationen, 180 Seiten A5

Blumen-Knigge 2100 Historisches, Mystisches, Festliches, Blumensprache, Umgang mit Blumen-Präsenten, 144 Seiten A5

Bekleidung! Ausdruck der Persönlichkeit – Lukas' Outfit-Knigge 2100, 196 Seiten A5

Nudel-Knigge 2100 Himmlische Teigwaren, 140 Seiten A5

Der Interkulturelle Kompetenz-Knigge 2100 Kultur, Kompetenz, Eindrücke – Gesten, Rituale, Zeitempfinden – Berichte, Tipps, Erlebnisse, 240 Seiten A5

China-Deutschland-Knigge 2100 Chinesen in Deutschland, 104 Seiten A5

Dschungel-Knigge 2100 Umgang in ungewohnter Umgebung, 192 Seiten A5

Von allen guten Geistern verlassen-Knigge 2100, 132 Seiten A5

Der Dicke-Knigge 2100 Aus dem prallen Leben des Dicken, 104 Seiten A5

Typisch Frau – Typisch Mann Knigge 2100 Unterschiede und Gemeinsamkeiten im Umgang mit dem anderen Geschlecht, 128 Seiten A5

Kulinarischer und Gastronomischer Knigge 2100 284 Seiten A5

Klo- und Pinkel-Knigge 2100 Vom privaten und öffentlichen Bedürfnis - Umgangsformen im Tabu-Bereich, 104 Seiten A5

Alles hat seine Zeit-Knigge 2100 Umgang mit der Zeit, 294 Seite A5

Omi hüpf' mal Märchen meiner Großmutter, Erlebnisse ihre Jugend und wahre Geschichten meines Vaters von und über Omi Rickchen, Hardcover, 312 Seiten

Der Hunde-Knigge 2100 Umgang mit dem Hund – Hundesprache – Der Hund in der Gesellschaft, 180 Seiten A5

Welcome to Germany-Knigge 2100 Umgangsformen, Verhaltensmuster und gesellschaftliches Miteinander im deutschsprachigen Europa, 108 Seiten A5

Besuch willkommen Knigge 2100 Einladung, Gast, Geschenk, Empfang, Feier, Gastfreundschaft, 200 Seiten A5

Leben, Tod und Ansichten Austausch mit Berühmtheiten über Wichtiges und Unwichtiges im Leben, 116 Seiten A5

Last List Leid 2100 Verlogene Welt?, 160 Seiten A5

Mensch Macht Mörder 2100 Verfall der Umgangsformen?, 260 Seiten A5

Tod, Trauer, Totenkult-Knigge 2100 Sterben, Trost, Takt, Bestatten, Tradition, Vorsorge, Tabus, Vergänglichkeit und Sonderbares, 212 Seiten A5

Corona-Knigge 2100 Umgang mit dem Virus, 88 Seiten 12x19, kartoniert

Das kleine Knigge-Quiz 2100 96 Seiten, 12x19 cm, kartoniert

Leben und Lifestyle

Rhetorik, Soft Skills, Hochschule, Beruf

Rhetorik ist Silber Von den ersten Schritten zu einer perfekten Präsentation, 336 Seiten A5, kartoniert, Zeichnungen

Moderation ist Gold Gesprächsführung, Umfragen, Talkrunden und Manipulation, 274 Seiten A5, kartoniert, Zeichnungen

Lebhafte Körpersprache in Vorträgen, Präsentationen, Gesprächen, 218 Seiten A5, kartoniert, ca. 290 Zeichnungen

Rhetoric – Mastering the Art of Persuasion, 222 Seiten A5, kartoniert

Discussion – Mastering the Skills of Moderation, 192 Seiten A5, kartoniert

Body Language in Europe, 196 Seiten A5, kartoniert, ca. 290 Zeichnungen

Das große Buch der Kommunikation und der Gesprächsführung [2100], 460 Seiten A5, kartoniert, Zeichnungen

Das große Buch der Rhetorik [2100] Tacheles reden; Präsentieren; manipulieren und überzeugen, 452 Seiten A5, kartoniert, viele Darstellungen

Trickreiche Rhetorik [2100] Psychologische Gesprächsführung, manipulierende Darstellung, unaufdringliches Nudging, 448 Seiten A5, kartoniert, Zeichnungen

Körpersprache [2100] **– Lüge, Verrat, Macht**, Im Beruf, vor Gericht, beim Flirt – Gewinnerpose und Demutshaltung; 440 Seiten A5, kartoniert, über 400 Zeichnungen

Soft Skills-Knigge [2100] Soziale, Persönlichkeit, Selbstmanagement, 480 Seiten A5, kartoniert, viele Darstellungen

Schlagfertigkeit-, Spontaneität-, Stegreif-Knigge [2100] Impulsiv handeln, verbale Angriffe kontern, Störungen entwaffnen, 104 Seiten A5

Pitch Skills und Überzeugungs-Knigge [2100] Elevator Pitch, Geldgeber beeindrucken, Feuer versprühen, 128 Seiten A5, kartoniert

Smalltalk-Knigge [2100] Vom kleinen Gespräch bis zum charmanten Flirt - Kontakt ausbauen, Sympathie zeigen, Begehrlichkeit wecken, 100 Seiten A5

Quassel-Knigge [2100] Quasseln, Quatschen, Quengeln oder Lebenswichtige Kommunikation – Gezielt eingesetzte Rhetorik – Aussagekräftiges Profil zeigen, 112 Seiten A5

Die moderne Führungskraft [2100] **Online und Präsenz,** Handbuch für souveräne Vorgesetzte und solche, die es werden wollen, 252 Seiten A5, kartoniert, Zeichnungen

Emotionale Rhetorik im Leben und rund um den Tod [2100] Vielfältige Kommunikation – Fiktiver Interview-Austausch mit Berühmtheiten, 260 Seiten A5

Innere Rhetorik [2100] Zielführende Kommunikation mit sich selbst, 140 Seiten A5

Kriegerische Rhetorik [2100] Sensible Diplomatie, einfühlsame Empathie, 156 Seiten A5

Blumige Rhetorik [2100] Zielführende Kommunikation mit sich selbst, 140 Seiten A5

Alles hat seine Zeit – Knigge [2100] Umgang mit der Zeit, 294 Seiten A5

Hochschul-Knigge [2100] Studentischer Umgang, 132 Seiten A5, kartoniert, Fotos

Jugend-Karriere-Knigge [2100] 224 Seiten A5, kartoniert, Zeichnungen, Checklisten

Bewerbungs-Knigge [2100] **für Frauen – Tina bewirbt sich / Bewerbungs-Knigge** [2100] **für Männer – Tom bewirbt sich,** Vorbereitung, Wahl der Kleidung, Verhalten beim Bewerbungsgespräch, je 128 Seiten A5, kartoniert, Fotos, Checklisten

Online-Bewerbungsgespräche-Knigge [2100] **Vorstellungsgespräche auf Distanz – Tina und Tom bewerben sich digital**, 128 Seiten A5, kartoniert, Zeichnungen

Kreativitäts-Knigge [2100], Visionärhaft denken, Scheuklappen sprengen, Mentales Risiko eingehen, 164 Seiten A5, kartoniert

Team und Typ-Knigge [2100], Ich und Wir, Typen und Charaktere, Team-Entwicklung, 128 Seiten A5, kartoniert, viele Darstellungen

Die flotte Generation Y im 21. Jahrhundert, selbstbewusst – lebensbetonend – flexibel, 116 Seiten A5, kartoniert, Zeichnungen

Die flotte Generation Z im 21. Jahrhundert, entscheidungsfreudig – effizient – eigenverantwortlich, 140 Seiten A5, kartoniert, Zeichnungen

Tele-Meeting [2100], Digitale Konferenz, Online-Unterricht, Homeoffice, 104 Seiten A5, kartoniert

Rhetorik, Soft Skills, Hochschule, Beruf

Englisch:

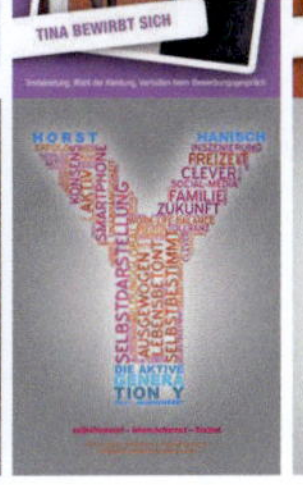

Beratung, Coaching, Seminar

Wer hat nicht gerne mit Menschen zu tun, die selbstbewusst und selbstsicher mit anderen Menschen umgehen?

Geschäftspartnern, die die elementaren Regeln des ‚Benimms' beherrschen, stehen die Türen zum Erfolg offen.

Unternehmen, die neben ihrer fachlichen Leistung auch ‚menschlich' überzeugen wollen, bieten wir für ihre Mitarbeiterinnen und Mitarbeiter aktives Training im Umgang mit Kunden, Gästen, Kollegen und Gesprächspartnern an.

Auf unserer Website informieren wir Sie über unsere Angebote:

- Firmen-Internes-Training
  → Business-Etikette und das Lehrmenü
  → Präsentieren, Moderieren, Kommunizieren
  → Körpersprache und ihre Geheimnisse
  → Teuflische Rhetorik und das Erkennen manipulativer Aspekte
  → Flottes Reden vor und zu anderen
  → Der erste entscheidende Eindruck
- Interkulturelles Training
  → Umgang mit Menschen anderer Kulturen
- Intensiv-Training für
  → TV-Auftritte
  → Vorträge
  → Präsentationen
  → Reden
- Fachliteratur und journalistische Beiträge
- Vorträge/Speaker
  → Vor kleinem und vor großem Publikum
- Workshops
  → Soft Skills
  → Team-Training

Individuelles Coaching für Einzelpersonen: Wer es ganz individuell mag, greift zurück auf ein Einzel-Coaching, auch als Online-Coaching. Hier werden ganz persönliche Herausforderungen angegangen, mit Themen wie:

- → Erscheinungsbild – Der Erste Eindruck
- → Selbstsicheres und authentisches Auftreten
- → Persönlichkeitsentfaltung
- → Bewerbungstraining
- → Rhetorik und Überzeugungskraft
- → Erfolgreiche Verhandlungsführung
- → Kommunikation und Konfliktbewältigung
- → Präsentations-Techniken und Moderation
- → Interkulturelle Kompetenz

und andere Themen – direkt auf die besonderen Bedürfnisse des Einzelnen zugeschnitten. Besuchen Sie uns auf www.knigge-seminare.de